# FORGIVENESS  AND  SUFFERING

T0382291

# FORGIVENESS AND SUFFERING

## A STUDY OF CHRISTIAN BELIEF

BY

DOUGLAS WHITE, M.D.

TRINITY COLLEGE, CAMBRIDGE

Cambridge:
at the University Press
1913

CAMBRIDGE UNIVERSITY PRESS
Cambridge, New York, Melbourne, Madrid, Cape Town,
Singapore, São Paulo, Delhi, Mexico City

Cambridge University Press
The Edinburgh Building, Cambridge CB2 8RU, UK

Published in the United States of America by Cambridge University Press, New York

www.cambridge.org
Information on this title: www.cambridge.org/9781107647343

© Cambridge University Press 1913

First published 1913
First paperback edition 2013

*A catalogue record for this publication is available from the British Library*

ISBN 978-1-107-64734-3 Paperback

TO MY WIFE

# PREFACE

THIS little book needs little introduction. It has been written in the hope of indicating a new point of view, at which the writer has himself arrived, but which he has not seen elsewhere described.

The chief conscious obligations, in respect of books, are acknowledged in the course of the essay; but perhaps immediate personal influences, which cannot be acknowledged, have a more permanent effect on the direction and development of thought than the mediate influence of books.

If some passages from one or more well-known works are selected for criticism, this is done in order to bring into relief the writer's own standpoint, not from any lack of respect for authors who are deservedly held in high esteem.

To Professor V. H. Stanton, Canon of Ely, who was good enough to read the MS and proofs, most hearty thanks are due for much helpful suggestion and kindly criticism: he must not, of course, be held responsible for the opinions expressed.

Other obligations, of a more private character, are better suited for private acknowledgement.

D. W.

Harrow-on-the-Hill,
*October* 1913.

# SYNOPSIS OF CONTENTS

## CHAPTER I

### THE PRESENT POSITION

## CHAPTER II

### LANDMARKS OF EARLIER THOUGHT

## CHAPTER III

### MODERN TENDENCIES

# CHAPTER IV

## NATURAL AND MORAL LAW

# CHAPTER V

## FORGIVENESS A PERSONAL RELATION

# CHAPTER VI

## THE NEED OF SUFFERING

of God a necessary outcome of Christian thought (**88**); no real
philosophic difficulty (**91**); self-limitation of God a necessity (**91**).
Self-sacrifice a joy; but contact with sin painful (**92**); forgiveness
not painful, yet reached through pain (**93**); God also is made perfect
through suffering (**94**).                                pp. 75—94

# CHAPTER VII

## FORGIVENESS VITAL NOT FORMAL

Transactions eliminated (**95**); God's attitude unaltered (**96**); the
"finished work" explained in accord with general sense of N.T. (**98**);
two objections met (**100**); "dereliction" discussed (**101—4**). Re-
capitulation (**105**); self-revelation God's purpose in Jesus (**106**); love,
suffering, forgiveness—a sequence (**107**).    Older and newer views
contrasted (**110**); Crucifixion represents an eternal truth (**113**); forgiveness the beginning, not the end; brings newness of life (**114**);
sacrifice and ensample (**115**); taking of manhood into God; only one
way of forgiveness (**116**).                             pp. 95—116

# CHAPTER VIII

## REFLECTIONS AND HOPES

A living picture (**117**).    Death of Christ not to be considered in
isolation (**118**); represents God's passion.    Potency of Christ's passion
not less real, though symbolical (**119**); value of this view to different
shades of belief (**120**); universal value of Passion, though in time
(**121**); importance of revised doctrine (**122**), as Christianising world
(**123**) and unifying Church (**124**).    Meaning of authority (**126**); recent
revolution of thought (**127**).                          pp. 117—128

# EPILOGUE

The City of God; its houses and citizens; a comparison.
                                                         pp. 129—133

# CHAPTER I

DIVINE forgiveness has always formed the central theme of religious thought, and must always so continue under man's existing condition of moral imperfection. It represents an instinctive need of man; springing from a sense that he is not what he ought to be, nor what God desires that he should be. It is not a specifically Christian conception, for the sense of need existed long before the Christian era. But Christianity did purport to offer and to provide a satisfaction of that need, which previous systems of religion had entirely failed to supply.

The desire for forgiveness is common to mankind; but the conceptions of forgiveness vary with the conceptions of God. Crude and unethical thoughts of God produce crude and unethical views of forgiveness. Always and everywhere these two things are necessarily interdependent. And if in the Christian church views have prevailed which are impossible for us now to accept, this is because the followers of Jesus have failed to imbibe the lofty and beautiful concept of God which he sought to impart. If we wish to reach a right understanding of the mind of Jesus on divine forgiveness, we can only succeed by setting ourselves to study his teaching about the nature of God.

The hindrance to right relations between man and God is two-fold; for not only do men feel a sense of moral degradation on their own side, but they are instinctively conscious of a divine antagonism; the need of moral recovery and that of personal reconciliation go hand in hand.

Christians in all ages have firmly believed that both the divine antagonism and the human degradation are done away by the sufferings of Christ; but their conceptions as to how this result is achieved have varied very widely, not only in the past but up to the present day. Thousands indeed have appropriated to themselves the benefits of the Christian religion, who have had the most primitive conceptions as to the manner in which these benefits become available, or as to the process of their assimilation; but at the present time the growing intelligence of a rising generation demands, more than ever before, some rational explanation of the doctrines which they are asked to believe; and to-day—I say it without hesitation—the current interpretations of the Christian doctrine of God's forgiveness are such as to raise a wellnigh insuperable barrier against the adoption of a definitely Christian form of thought among men of average intelligence.

I do not suggest that out-and-out Calvinism is believed or taught by the clergy of the present day, still less that it is accepted by the laity. Yet it must be admitted that the mode of thought which produced Calvinism is still at work to-day; satisfaction theories are still dominant, though the form in which they are presented has been greatly modified. It may be doubted whether it has even occurred to the majority of present-day Christians that there can be any alternative.

The doctrine of penal substitution, introduced at the Reformation, has few supporters at present; but while there is a general desire to avoid this presentation, the usual tendency is to alter its form rather than its substance ; it is still assumed that some form of satisfaction to God was necessary which man was powerless to render. But what sort of satisfaction was required, or how it has been rendered, is left indeterminate. In the pulpit, indeed, there is a tendency to say as little as possible on the subject. Enough must be said, on the one hand, to show that belief in the doctrine of Atonement is still alive; on the other, it is not desired to disturb the faith of the older members of congregations by setting forth a new explanation ; and, even in the case of the younger members, there is a fear of depriving their minds of one form of belief before another can be assimilated—a fear, as it were, of pruning the tree too early, and exposing it to the danger of frost. Both these fears are ill-founded ; it is, after all, not so easy to disturb the settled opinions of elderly people ; and as for the younger persons, they are already exposed to doubts and questionings of a more radical kind than their elders commonly suspect ; the pressing need is that these early misgivings should be frankly met and openly dealt with.

Yet, while timidity of innovation to some

extent explains the lack of virile teaching in the modern pulpit, there is a much more potent cause; namely, that while the theory of penal substitution was from many points of view unsatisfactory, it was at least definite; and, as yet, no very definite theory has grown up to replace it. Modern thought on the subject has not yet crystallised; it has assumed no concise, pictorial form to the minds of the clergy themselves; and if the teacher's thought be misty and undefined, it is hardly likely to leave a sharp impression on the mind of the scholar.

To this it is commonly replied, "No cut-and-dried theory of the Atonement can be truly satisfactory; we are dealing with a mystery which the human mind cannot grasp in its entirety; it is like the sun to the human eye; we can see its effulgence only, we cannot discern its substance." Are we then to abstain from forming a big, comprehensive conception of God's attitude towards us? Has He given us the capacity of asking large and, as it seems to us, vital questions as regards our relations to Him, yet barred us at the start from ever answering them? Christian thought must be progressive, if it is to escape the risk of becoming obsolete.

Again, we are told that it is more profitable for a Christian to contemplate, now from one aspect, now from another, the marvels of God's grace, than to form any theory by which it can be brought down to the level of our understanding; we reverence most that which is beyond our grasp. This is the plea of many a reverent and thoughtful soul; and yet I think that even this too may be wrong. Think: when did you begin to look with most wondering eyes at the glories of the star-lit sky, the sun, the moon, and all the host of heaven? Was it before or after you had made an attempt to understand and appreciate the workings of the solar system? Did a knowledge of the laws and relations of the heavenly bodies diminish your wonderment at God's creative power? The question, I think, admits of but one answer. The further our mind penetrates the mysteries of nature, the more wonderful they become; the more we come to know, the wider is the expanse of the unknown, and the greater the marvel of the partly known.

As with the material universe, so is it with our world of personalities, and so with our conceptions of God. As we understand Him

better, and think of Him more truly, the greater
by far will be our reverence for His sublimity,
our trust in His faithfulness, and our adoration
of His love. For myself, I confess, what I crave
is a glimpse, a bird's-eye view, if you will, as
from a distance, of the Divine System, not
the less spiritual because intellectual : as we
might see the city of London as a whole from
high above it ; not that we do not wish to abide
in the City—whether it be the city of London
or the city of God—but that having seen it in
its totality, though imperfectly, we might the
better henceforth appreciate its details as por-
tions of the whole. It is this very craving to
grasp things as a whole, which has wrought
the revolutions of science ; which has plucked
observed facts from their dreary isolation of
pigeon-holes, and placed them, like coloured
pieces, in the beautiful harmony of Nature's
picture ; which has taken men, and dates, and
battles, and by the magic of a master-thought
has turned them into history ; which has made
the crust of the earth declare its own story, and
coaxed their secrets from the stars.

All these things we know but in part ; each
answer of nature leads on to further questions,

which in turn draw their own response. So also must be our faith in the world which transcends material things—that to a vital question there must somewhere be an answer sufficient for us; that when we knock at the door of knowledge, it will not remain closed to us for ever. Here also, as in other quests, our objective is Truth; to find Truth, we must face our problem squarely, undeterred by any mistaken sense of reverence. If a conception be false, it were best unmasked. Truth will survive handling; it may be buried out of sight for a time; but it is alive, and will presently shoot up, green and fresh, from the soil which has hidden it. In such a spirit of frank but serious optimism, I invite my readers to enter with me into a short study of a great problem.

# CHAPTER II

IT is impossible, and unwise if it were possible, to embark on such a quest without a glance[1] at the various solutions of the problem which have been offered in the past. Men have not always thought as they think now. Theories quite different from that of penal substitution have been advanced, claiming scriptural support; and so large is the thought-range of the apostolic age, that even the most diverse and irreconcileable theories might seem to find some justification in one or other of the New Testament writings. All the great authors abound in figures of speech through which they seek to convey their thought; but their conceptions are wider than the figures which illustrate them. Each writer speaks in the terms of his own mental upbringing, so long as such terms seem

---

[1] Throughout this chapter my acknowledgements are due to H. N. Oxenham's *Catholic Doctrine of the Atonement*, and G. B. Stevens's *Christian Doctrine of Salvation*.

adequate ; St Paul in terms of Jewish Law, the writer to the Hebrews in terms of the ritual of Hebrew sacrifice ; but each of them confessedly finds his own terminology inadequate. The Law is but the nursemaid who brings pupils to the school of Christ ; the sacrifices are not the real things but only a dim shadow of the reality. Christian thought indeed is like the daffodil; its bud is at first enclosed in a flower-case ; but as the bud expands, the flower-case has done its protective work, and is thrown off.  So with these writers; their thought could not keep within the limits of its early expression; as the one expanded, the other passed into obsolescence.

In thus suggesting that the writers of the apostolic age did not mean to tie themselves up to any theory of Atonement, I know that I am on debated ground ; but when once we leave the apostolic, and pass to the sub-apostolic age, the case is different.  There certainly we find an entire absence of any definite theory ; and so things remained during the greater part of the second century.  Not that the matter was absent from the mind of Christians of that period ; it was indeed the subject of devout meditation and beautiful utterance, as the Epistle to

Diognetus may exemplify ; but their pearls of thought were unstrung; they had no consciously formulated theory ; their faith was simple ; as yet there was no demand for an intellectual system.

One thing, however, bulked large in religious thought of that time, which was destined to give both colour and shape to Christian theory for many a long year; this was the Personality of the Devil, the Prince of this world, who held and exercised practical sway over the wills of men. In the dominance of this belief, it was natural that the work of Christ should figure as a personal triumph over Satan. And so this idea gradually asserts itself, till it finds free expression, but not full explanation, in the writings of Irenaeus (bp. of Lyons 178—202). Its development was left for the restless creative genius of Origen (fl. 204—253), the greatest Christian thinker of that age, whose versatile imagination was free from the yet unknown trammels of authority. The theory of redemption which he laid down fails indeed to meet our modern needs ; even to Origen himself, judging from the rest of his work, it must have appeared as only a partial explanation of the truth; yet it was destined to hold the theoretic field, not indeed exclusively, but predominantly, for nearly a thousand years. By his scheme of thought the redemption of man was effected by means of a compact or bargain between God and the Devil; and we must confess that, even regarded as a commercial transaction, it is by no means above ethical criticism.  Mankind, by this theory, were under the dominion of Satan, who held over them the powers, if not the rights, of slave-ownership.  Having acquired these powers not by force but by the consent of man, it was right that, if men were to be freed from the bondage, an equivalent price should be paid to the Devil; and this price, which God alone was able to pay, was nothing else than the death of Christ.  But although the compact was struck, Satan did not realise what he was doing; not only did he overlook the influence which the life and death of Christ would exercise upon man, but he failed to perceive that, having compassed Christ's death, he could not hold the soul of Christ, which was superior to death; by the resurrection, therefore, Satan was in effect cheated of the product of his bargain.

Thus by his ignorance the Devil compassed his own downfall; of this ignorance God took full advantage, and paid back Satan in his own coin.

To the modern mind the picture is grotesque, quite apart from ethical considerations. That God should hold traffic with the Devil is to us inconceivable. But the chief reason for this is that, unlike our forefathers, we no longer believe in a personal Devil. We believe, indeed (who does not?), in personal influences, which are all about us, both for good and evil; but the embodiment of evil in the person of a Devil, ranking in power second only to the good God —this is a belief which we no longer share. In spite, however, of so great a change in thought, we may note that this sort of belief has not yet wholly vanished; even to-day from pulpit and platform you may hear explanations of the Atonement which, in the last resort, involve the same conception[1].

[1] In this context cp. Hymns A. & M. 96, *v.* 5:
> Upon its arms (the cross) like balance true,
> He weigh'd the price for sinners due,
> The price which none but He could pay,
> *And spoiled the spoiler of his prey.*

Is this an echo of the patristic view, or only an adaptation of Lc. xi. 21 (=Mc. iii. 27, Mt. xii. 29. The strong man armed)?

Having outlined Origen's theory of redemption, I should be ill serving my readers if I left them with the impression that this was all that Origen had to say. His teaching in truth is full of spirituality; he dwells insistently on personal reconciliation with God, purification of life, and the permanent value of Christ's perfect manhood. At present, however, we have to deal with his formal theory of redemption; and its defects, from a modern standpoint, need no emphasizing. Yet the Christian world, as a whole, acquiesced in that view for many centuries; not that everybody accepted it, but it was never formally demolished till nearly 1100 A.D. Passing on, therefore, to that date, our scene changes from Alexandria to Canterbury; and the gracious figure of Anselm challenges our attention.

In the person of Anselm were combined statesman, saint, and scholar; if Origen gave form and system to the theology of the Fathers, Anselm heralds the advent of Scholastic thought. In him for the first time we find the hypothesis of a compact with Satan formally abrogated. For Anselm, indeed, the personal Devil still exists, but not as disputing sovereignty with

God. How (he asks) could the Devil have any rights at all in God's world ? God owed the Devil nothing at all except punishment, and all the more that he had deceived man, and so lured him from the path of goodness. It was not God who had to make any recompense to the Devil, but man who had to make a recompense to God. Man by his sin had violated the order of the world, and by the same act had personally affronted God ; not only must the lost balance be restored, but the offended honour of God must be satisfied. Now (so thinks Anselm) owing to man's sinfulness neither of these objects can be achieved by him ; he already owes to God the homage of his life ; even if this were perfectly rendered, it could not atone for the sinful past ; something further is required, which must be rendered by man, and yet which is beyond man's power to supply. The need is supplied by Jesus, the God-Man. He is able both to restore the lost order, and to satisfy the offended honour of God. True, he too, as man, owed God the homage of his life ; but, being sinless, he did not pass under the sinner's sentence of death. His death, therefore, freely offered to God, was of such infinite value as not only to balance the moral deficit, but also to give satisfaction to the Creator for the personal affront. Thus reconciliation with God has been achieved, without any breach of the moral order of the universe.

Sin, then, is an affront to God. Influenced[1], no doubt, by the environment of his own age, Anselm attributed to God something of the qualities of a great feudal baron; affronted by sin, He requires some personal satisfaction; since man is incapable of rendering this unaided, God graciously makes it possible by means of the Incarnation.

The negative side of Anselm's argument obtained a speedy acceptance; though combated by Bernard, it was admitted by Abelard; the death of Christ was no longer accepted by Christendom in the sense of a compact with the Devil. His positive theory, however, profoundly as it influenced the whole Scholastic age, failed to command the general assent; into the reasons for this failure it is not possible here to enter; to the modern mind one reason is sufficient. The argument depends entirely

[1] See Stevens, *Christian Doctrine of Salvation*, p. 241.

on the postulate that physical death is the penalty or result of sin. Take this away and the whole formal structure of the theory collapses.

To judge rightly, however, of Anselm's contributions to thought (and they were many) we must throw ourselves back into his age and understand his relation to it.

It is, indeed, hardly possible for any modern thinker to accept his conclusions in the form in which he moulded them ; yet his work was in advance of contemporary thought ; it fulfilled adequately the theological requirements of his own age, and offered fresh food for thought to his successors ; he had turned the stream of theological thought into an entirely new channel. And if, after the lapse of another 800 years we have ceased to feel the direct influence of his speculation, we must still remember how great a boon he conferred on Christian thought by his destruction of the unethical theory of a compact with Satan. But more than this too. For if his positive theory was inadequate, yet it contained elements of truth which were capable of exerting, and did exert, a beneficent influence on future thought.

His, indeed, was the first theoretic advancement of a satisfaction rendered to God; but it is a superficial view which sees in him the father of the Reformation theories; these, I think, would have repelled Anselm almost as much as they repel us. Indeed, strange as it may sound, I suspect that the undercurrent[1] of Anselm's thought was more in line with modern ideas than with those of the Reformation; for, after his own fashion, he was the first to express two important things; first, the conception of what I may call the moral equilibrium of the universe; and secondly, the personal sensitiveness of God towards sin. The terms, indeed, in which that sensitiveness are expressed are unfortunate, being coloured by the social conditions of his own day; yet it was something to have perceived it at all. As we proceed, we shall see the significance to ourselves of these two ideas, although they need modern interpretation and handling.

The name of Anselm ushers in the age of the Schoolmen. Into their systems of thought we cannot here enter. Was the life and death

---

[1] It is unjust, I think, to label Anselm's theory "commercial." The thought of equilibrium invites commercial illustration, in the sense of balancing accounts; but the thought runs deeper than its illustration.

of Christ an absolute necessity for man's salvation, or could God have found another way? Was the Incarnation devised as a remedy for man's sin alone, or was it a necessary step in the gradual perfection of the human race, irrespective of sin? Both these questions are of deep interest. By their opposite answers to the latter, Thomas Aquinas and Duns Scotus sowed the seeds of two conflicting tendencies of modern theology. Yet such questions are not on the direct line of our present study; we must pass on to the sixteenth century, in which thought again becomes creative rather than contemplative.

By the Reformers, "sin is viewed as a "violation of God's inexorable law, and not "merely as an affront to His honour. The "necessity which now arises is not merely "a necessity to vindicate His majesty; it is the "necessity that sin be punished. It is no "longer a question of God's dignity or honour, "but of His inflexible justice. It is no longer, "as with Anselm, a question of satisfaction *or* "punishment, but of satisfaction *by* punish- "ment. If therefore sin is to be forgiven, "it must, first of all, be punished[1]." This

[1] Stevens, *Christian Doctrine of Salvation*, p. 152.

is the essence of the Reformation view, of which Luther and Calvin are the chief, but not the only, exponents. The revolt of Socinus (1539—1604) from this doctrine, is of interest, not only in itself, but as leading up to the theory of Grotius (1583—1645). Socinus maintained (with Anselm) that sin, indeed, is an affront to the majesty of God ; but he also propounded that it is perfectly competent for God to forgive the affront, if He so pleases, without punishment. He condemns as impossible the theory of penal substitution, which he also considers superfluous. Indeed, for him, the necessity of Christ's death disappears entirely, in so far as it is regarded as a basis for the forgiveness of sins. The declaration of Socinus, in fact, constituted a powerful challenge to the whole system of current orthodoxy.

The challenge thus thrown down, is taken up by Grotius, the lawyer, in a somewhat unexpected manner. He answers that God is the Governor of the world, and that He must govern on principles of righteousness. The abrogation of the right to exact satisfaction for sin would produce chaos, although such a right need not be exercised in every case.

God's right to exact satisfaction was exhibited in the death of Christ—whose mission to earth is, on this view, regarded as a sort of armed demonstration of the rights and righteousness of God. God need not indeed exact from every man satisfaction equivalent to his sin ; but He must do something to maintain the moral order of the world which He governs. He must, to use the modern useful but elusive phrase, *vindicate* His righteousness. In view of this necessity, a striking example is required ; this character Christ voluntarily undertakes, and thus exhibits to the world the terrible consequences of sin, in order that man may in future choose the path of righteousness. Grotius does not consider that Christ paid the penalty of man's sin, but that he exemplified it. The obvious answer to this proposition is that, if the Governor is to uphold law and order, he can only do so by punishing the guilty ; if a dreadful example be regarded as necessary, the choice for that purpose of an innocent person is singularly infelicitous.

Grotius, then, occupied a middle position between those who affirmed that God can and does forgive without punishment, and those who declared that God is bound by the inner necessity of His nature, to inflict penalty with the full rigour of the offended law. But this half-way house was not suited to be a permanent resting-place of thought, particularly at such a time; and already, when the theory of Grotius was put forward, theological opinion, under the powerful influence of the leaders of the Reformation, was steadily setting in the direction of punishment with full rigour, as a necessary preliminary to forgiveness.

This view, namely, that God is bound by the eternal justice of His nature, to exact from mankind the full penalties of sin, had been already declared in no doubtful terms. Luther (1483—1546) boldly plunged into the theory from which all previous theologians had shrunk : God, being driven by the inherent law of His nature to punish sin to its full desert, had graciously provided a substitute for the sinner in the person of His Son ; on this innocent victim He wreaked the full vengeance due for sin, thus balancing the account between sinners and God. Jesus thus endured the penalty of our sins upon the cross ; and as that penalty involved damnation, Calvin does not stick at saying that Christ endured the pains of hell. This is in fact the unadulterated theory of penal substitution.

How such a theory can ever have been acceptable to the human mind it is hard to understand ; one can only think that some such drastic restatement was needed to countervail the conception, then no doubt widely prevalent, of a benevolent Deity, whose good nature shrank from the necessary exercise of moral discipline.

But the scheme of Luther will not stand examination any more than its predecessors ; philosophically it is as unsound as the others ; ethically it is repellent. Granted that God is eternally just, granted that justice must exact the full penalty of sin ; then every sinner must himself bear in full the penalty of his own sin. The term penalty is meaningless apart from its correlative, guilt ; an innocent man cannot endure penalty for a guilty man, any more than he can appropriate his guilt. Nor are matters improved by the voluntary character assigned to Christ's sufferings. To suffer voluntarily on behalf of another, to risk or lose life or health in order to save another—this is vicarious suffering, which we know and understand ;

vicarious penalty, substitutionary punishment, is outside the range of our experience or thought. Its advocates suggest the analogy of an innocent child, ready and willing to receive a beating from his father in the place of his guilty brother; but the father who could thus satisfy his appetite for vengeance has yet to be found even in this imperfect world. And if it sometimes happens, in the administration of the law of the land, that the innocent suffers for the guilty, this is only a miscarriage of justice, and does not in the slightest degree satisfy the majesty of the offended law[1].

The whole conception of penal substitution depends for its validity on the presumed isolability of the sin from the sinner, as if it were a *thing* separable from a *person*, very much as my hat might be removed from my head, and placed on another's. But sin is not in this way transferable; guilt is a strictly personal burden,

[1] Under cover of such analogies as these, the doctrine of penal substitution may be presented in a less unattractive form; as for instance in one of the *Hymns for Infant Minds*, by A. & J. Taylor (1876):

> He knew how wicked men had been,
> And knew that God must punish sin ;
> So out of pity Jesus said
> He'd bear the punishment instead.

which can in no way be shifted on to another's shoulders. Indeed, if we use the word burden, it is the burden of a disease, a deformity, a cancer. What is required is not an outward transference, but an inward cure. Here, then, is the first flaw in the doctrine of penal substitution, that neither guilt nor its correlative, punishment, are transferable; so that, if it is necessary to inflict punishment at all, it must be inflicted on the person of the guilty and on no one else. But even if this elementary difficulty could be eliminated, the theory of penal substitution does not even square with the facts which it seeks to explain. It is claimed that, inasmuch as the wages of sin is death, Christ by his death paid in full the penalty due to man's sin. But what is meant by death in this connexion? No one can now believe that *physical* death is the result of sin; moreover, if physical death be the penalty of sin, then Christ's death does not in fact save us from this penalty. But did Christ then suffer *eternal* death, commonly called damnation, in order to save us from that penalty? Obviously not. So it is not clear, to say the least, in what sense Christ did in fact endure the penalty due to mankind, any more than it is clear philosophically how punishment can be transferred from the guilty to the innocent.

If the doctrine of penal substitution be supposed to exhibit the love of God, it does so at the expense of even a show of justice; if it exhibits the justice of God, then, since justice requires forgiveness, there is left no room for love.    The difficulties are overwhelming.

Add to all this that there is not in the life or in the death of Jesus a single suggestion that he was conscious of the wrath or displeasure of the Father.    The constant love, trust, and obedience of Jesus, throughout his life and death, carries with it, as its necessary reciprocal, the love, tenderness and good-pleasure of the Heavenly Father; whereas a penal interpretation of his sufferings involves the idea of strained relations, and postulates displeasure, separation, aversion.    I am aware that in certain quarters such an interpretation is still upheld, mainly on the ground of two utterances of Jesus himself; with this contention I propose to deal later on in detail (p. 100 ff.).    But for the present no one will deny that throughout the gospel history, Jesus is represented, not only as acting, speaking, and thinking, in absolute harmony with the divine will, but as being himself conscious of the Father's perfect sympathy, favour and coöperation ; the authority which he claimed was in virtue of his intimate personal understanding of the Father's will (Mt. xi. 27, Lc. x. 22) ; the chief reason of the Father's love was his very willingness to lay down his life (Jo. x. 17). In face of such a picture of harmony, we are asked to believe that in his death-agony all this was altered : his Father's face turned away in displeasure ; the union broken ; the love turned into antipathy. It is incredible ; such a view of things turns the life of Christ into a monstrous historical anomaly.

Lastly, we must not leave the doctrine of penal substitution without noticing a further difficulty which it raises. For if it grates on the philosophical and historical sense, it is no less shocking to the theological mind. The Christian doctrine presupposes absolute unity of will and action between the Father and the Son ; the Son's abode is in the bosom of the Father ; he is the express image of the Father's person ; whatever the Father does, that also does the Son. Separation, punishment, wrath,

—such terms are the language of flat ditheism; to a monotheist, incarnation can only be a self-expression of God, whereby, as in a mirror, He reveals His nature and character to man ; any thought of collision, friction, disharmony, between God and his self-expression is unthinkable ; and not less so from the stand-point of Trinitarian theology than from any other. Whatever distinctions may be conceivable within the Divine nature, these cannot be subversive of the unity in which they are rooted; distinction of will, purpose, aim, cannot be allowed. Monotheism is the first axiom of Christianity. It is a thing much to be remembered.

# CHAPTER III

In the foregoing chapter we have passed in brief review the chief guises in which, up to the Reformation period, the doctrine of the Atonement was presented. We have seen God as a Conqueror, triumphing over the Devil; we have seen God as a feudal Baron, affronted by the action of his vassals, yet willing to accept a suitable reparation; we have seen God as Governor keeping order within His domain by means of an exemplary severity, which "vindicates" his holiness; lastly we have seen God as Judge, meting out to mankind the full and just reward of their evil deeds, but mercifully substituting another to bear their penalty. Between these various presentments, there are striking differences; yet underlying those differences, there is an important similarity.

They differ, in that by the theory of Luther

there is an inherent necessity in the nature of God to punish before He can forgive; the amount of punishment must exactly balance the offence. With the other schemes, the amount of satisfaction exacted is just so much as God is pleased to be satisfied with. In the latter case He is an arbiter, who can say " It is enough; stay now thine hand"; in the former, He is a judge, simply administering a law over which He has no control.

In the earlier theology God is able freely to determine both the quantity and the quality of such satisfaction as He demands; whatever He pleases to accept cannot but be just, seeing that Himself has ordered it. This, to the modern mind, is acceptable enough, so far as it goes; but, while it leaves the will of God free, it also leaves unexplained the principles on which the will of God is exercised. By Luther's theology, on the contrary, God is bound by a fixed scale of judicial equivalence, which He is powerless to abrogate or even to modify. Here the underlying principle is clear enough, however unpleasant it may seem; but we cannot insist too much, that if there be an absolute law, compelling God to punish sin, then by that law the guilty must be punished, and no substitute can avail.

The difficulty, indeed, of the doctrine of penal substitution was perceived at an early period ; and an attempt was made to circumvent it by setting up the analogy of debt. Now it is obvious that a debtor may have his debt paid by another, with satisfaction to both debtor and creditor ; but if we rest on the financial analogy, it is also obvious that the matter may be solved another way, namely, by the creditor remitting the debt. Moreover, we cannot help noticing that when Jesus employed the analogy of debt (as he did) he portrayed God as acting by remission, and not by substitution. "When they had nothing to pay, he frankly forgave them both." So that the analogy of debt seems to controvert the very thesis which it was intended to support.

But if there are many and wide differences between the views of Origen, Anselm, Grotius, and Luther, there is still between them all an essential similarity. They are all engaged in explaining how God overcame a difficulty. The difficulty is variously presented, and is solved in various ways. But it is always really the

same difficulty; and it lies within the being
of God. These theologians are all dealing with
a supra-mundane transaction which, in the first
instance at least, lies entirely outside of man's
ethical coöperation; not that the thought of
any of these reformers was really unethical;
but their expressed theories, while admitting
of ethical and spiritual adjuncts, were yet in
themselves, so far as man was concerned,
neither ethical nor spiritual. By all these
writers, the remission of sins is regarded as
being completed, as it were, " in vacuo," without reference and in no relation to the persons
who are to be forgiven; it is now felt—and
very properly felt—that if forgiveness of sins
is to be a spiritual reality, it must from the
outset come into closer and more immediate
contact with the human soul than these explanations imply.

All transactional theories are primarily
objective[1]. They spend their main energy,

[1] There is at the present time a tendency to deprecate the
use of the words "objective" and "subjective," on the ground
that neither has any content of meaning apart from the other.
This thesis is elaborated by Dr R. C. Moberly (*Atonement and
Personality*, Ch. VII.); and Dr Stevens sympathizes with this
contention, in so far as these terms are open to abuse and

that is to say, in defining the effect which
the sufferings of Jesus produced upon the mind
of God, how they enabled God to square justice
with mercy, and how thereafter it was possible
for man to obtain forgiveness. The subjective
aspect of the matter,—namely, the effect produced on man, and the reception by man of
the proffered salvation—this occupies quite a
subsidiary position in such speculation. Accordingly, the later exponents of the penal-
substitution theory have attempted to ethicise
it, to bring it down to the sphere of its human
operation ; to show how the death of Christ

misconstruction (*Christian Doctrine of the Atonement*, p. 257). We
can indeed have no sympathy with those who deride ethical or
emotional views of this doctrine on the ground that they are
"purely subjective," as if subjective perception of a truth could
exist apart from its objective validity. On the other hand,
Dr Moberly seems equally to insist that in the death of Christ
there was, not only an exhibition of the real (objective) attitude
of God towards sinners, but also a definite *fait accompli*, a thing
actually accomplished, awaiting indeed the perception of men,
but completed nevertheless independently of their perception
of it. While therefore in the perception of truth, "objective"
and "subjective" are each meaningless apart from the other,
there is still much room for disagreement as to the content of
the objective truth; and here Dr Moberly seems really to fall
into line with the earlier rather than with the more modern
school of theology.

is calculated to bring home to men's consciences
the grievousness of evil-doing, and turn them
from sin to righteousness. Having shown the
effect which Christ's death exercised on God,
they now proceeded to show the effect which
it ought to have on man.

But, while the importance of the manward
aspect of Christ's death was looming larger in
the thoughts of devout men, they were also
being increasingly impressed with the philosophic difficulties of penal substitution. Calvinism began to be watered down, or even to be
laid aside, in favour of less harsh views, often
more or less approximating to the milder, less
rigid schemes of Anselm or Grotius.

It was inevitable that in the nineteenth
century religious thought should transfer itself
from the speculative to the practical sphere.
Accordingly we find, specially in the last half-
century, the conception of penal substitution
passing into obsolescence, while attention is
concentrated on Jesus's perfect life of self-
sacrifice, his entire union of heart with the
Father, and his overpowering appeal to the
hearts of men. If (it is urged) God so loved
the world as to send His Son, then surely He

was already reconciled to men; He already loved them, and needed not to be warmed into love by any sacrifice. Thus the conception has become what is usually termed subjective, its objective part (as hitherto conceived) having been dismissed as either unimportant or untrue. The death of Christ, by this view, possesses an attractive and absorbing influence on the mind of man, drawing him up to God; but it neither exercises, nor did ever exercise, any influence over God, by way of propitiation or alteration of His attitude towards men. The love of God, as exhibited in Christ, is eternal; Christ is its expression, not its cause. Thus the modern conception of redemption has become an ethical one; mathematical, legal, and official analogies have become obsolescent. The love of Christ redeems the world, by drawing men into the paths of holiness and self-sacrifice. Redemption has become, for us, a "spiritual process" rather than "a superhuman transaction"[1]; we prefer to emphasize the truths of Divine Immanence, and to leave alone the fantastic transcendentalism

[1] J. M. Wilson, *The Gospel of the Atonement*, p. 146. No student can afford to miss this book, which consists of the Hulsean lectures for 1898.

of a bygone age; to ponder over the relation of God with the human soul, rather than to speculate on the internal mysteries of the Divine nature.

From the above-sketched point of view, much has been written which is beautiful, spiritual, invigorating, and above all, true. And yet I feel that it is not the whole truth. It fails to satisfy, because it leaves unanswered certain vital questions. Why was it that "Christ must needs suffer"? What is the meaning of this necessity of suffering ($\delta\epsilon\hat{\iota}$ $\pi\alpha\theta\epsilon\hat{\iota}\nu$) so often referred to in the Gospels and Acts[1]? If it be answered, "We admit that it was necessary that Christ should suffer, though we cannot see the reason why; the mysterious necessity of suffering, not for Christ alone, but for ourselves also, obtrudes itself upon our notice; we must accept for a fact what we cannot fathom with our understanding," I reply, If Christ died for our sins, then it is a fact of ultimate importance. To abandon its interpretation is to give up the main struggle of theology; it is a counsel of despair,

[1] Mt. xvi. 21, Mc. viii. 31, Lc. ix. 22, xvii. 25, xxiv. 7, 26, 46 [Jo. iii. 14, xii. 34], Ac. xvii. 3.

a confession of failure. The meaning of Christ's sufferings is the very nucleus of the Christian system. At the least we must have a working theory of it, something round which we can weave our thought. As long as people could accept one or other of the older interpretations, so long they had an intellectual background to their faith ; it formed an anchorage to their mind, so long as the anchor held ; but now, for us, the anchorage has failed, and it is felt that we are drifting on a sea of doubtful speculation, while the tide of modern tendency is setting steadily towards the shoals of pantheism. It is in the hope of pointing to a better anchorage that this book is written ; it can only succeed, if it helps towards a clearer and truer conception not only of the Divine dealings with man, but of the Divine Being Himself. The doctrine of Divine Immanence alone will not satisfy the mind. There is still a theology, as well as a mythology, of Divine Transcendence.

# CHAPTER IV

## NATURAL AND MORAL LAW

BEFORE we can get a clear view of our subject, we must have a sharp conception of what we mean by the terms in which we express ourselves. Certain terms always enter into the discussion of this problem, which lead to hopeless confusion because of ambiguity in their meaning; such words are Law, Punishment, Evil.

What, for instance, do we mean by Law? We speak of the laws of nature and of the moral law[1]; the use of the same word blinds us to the fact that we are talking of two things which not only are dissimilar, but do not even belong to the same category of thought. Not uncommonly you may hear a preacher say: "The laws of nature recoil with certainty on the man who disobeys them; so God's moral law will certainly recoil on the disobedient; be sure your sin will find you out." It sounds

[1] I use the term "moral law" in its ordinary sense, as summarizing the dictates of the moral conscience.

well, but it is a double untruth. The laws of
nature are statements of sequences which always
happen; of particular forces which always and
everywhere produce a certain result. You
cannot disobey, cannot even think of disobey-
ing, a law of nature; it is self-acting. An
architect may build a bridge not strong enough
to support the train which is to cross it; his
wrong calculation may result in death and
destruction. But he has not broken the law
of nature. The law has acted; the bridge, the
train, the architect's reputation, have all been
broken; the only thing which is not broken
is the law of action and reaction. You can
neither break these laws, tamper with them,
nor dodge them; they are self-acting, always
and everywhere. We conquer nature not by
obeying it, but by understanding it; it is even
a solecism to talk of obeying the laws of nature;
for we have no choice; the laws are merely
compendious statements of fact. The moral
law is widely different; this consists of what is
termed the moral imperative; it may be to
some extent codified and externalized, as in
the decalogue; yet the reason why it com-
mands the consciences of men is that it comes

not from without, but from within. But here men have the power of disobedience; "Thou shalt" may be countered by "I will not," "Thou shalt not" by "I shall."

Thus by the word "Law" we express two widely different conceptions; so different that it is hard to see between them any point of contact; they seem almost to occupy separate planes of thought.

Perhaps the origin of the confusion may be traced to that poetic license, whereby the inanimate creation is represented as obeying the behests of the Creator, as if endowed with consciousness. Examples of this abound in the Psalms, as, for instance, in Ps. civ., where the whole creation is pictured as waiting on the Divine command. These are figures of speech, and as such possess both beauty and value; but both are destroyed by the advent of literalism. The sea and tides work in accordance with the Divine will; to suggest that they *obey* the Divine will is to use a figure of speech; for the word obedience, if literally used, implies possible disobedience. So also, if we talk of human beings obeying the laws of nature, we must remember that the expression

is a loose one ; for there is really no question of
obedience or disobedience ; the laws are self-
acting.   Man's moral life, on the contrary, is
wholly taken up with obedience or disobedience
to the dictates of his conscience ; moral life is
a continual choice.   It would appear then as
if natural law and moral law are so different in
their nature and scope as to have nothing in
common ; they are not only different, they are
hardly even comparable.   One is tempted, indeed, to wonder whether they have any relation
to each other, operating as they do on different
planes of thought and experience.

Yet, widely distinct as are the two senses of
the single word " Law," there is a connecting
link between the two ; for the regulations of
society are based on the experience of nature.
The child is taught by its mother not to do
certain things, because she knows that certain
results will happen ; if the child plays with
fire, it will be burned ; if it eats unripe fruit,
indigestion will ensue ; if it tells a lie, the
results of that lie will affect both child and
mother.   Thus there are fixed laws (natural
sequences) in respect of inorganic nature, in
respect of physiology, in respect of social and

moral relations; and the laws (ordinances) of the family, society and state, are based on a recognition of the natural laws in their various spheres of operation.

The laws of gravitation include in their scope all nature, inorganic and organic, living and lifeless; gravity conditions the lives of plants and animals as well as their environment. Yet, while these laws give condition to the life and movement of all living things, they cannot be said to hamper such movements. We cannot follow, for instance, the eminent author[1] who has spoken of flowers growing "in the teeth of gravity," as if gravity were a crushing force against which the flower has to struggle. Gravity is a necessary condition of the flower's upward growth; without gravity, there were no upwards. Similarly all our own movements and actions are conditioned by gravity; gravity conditions the education of the senses which direct those actions—muscular sense, sense of position, sense of weight. Hence it is absurd to talk of any action of ours as "in defiance of the laws of nature"; for the fixity and self-activity of

[1] Henry Drummond, *Natural Law in the Spiritual World*, p. 131 (13th ed.).

nature's laws are the basis of all our physical and intellectual life and progress.

But besides such laws of universal application, there are other laws which embrace in their scope vital processes as distinct from non-vital. Thus there is the law of action and reaction between the bodily powers of man and the poisons which may enter his system. The advent of certain germs will cause his system to react in certain ways; through such experience of action and reaction we discover the laws (general principles) of health and disease. When these laws are sufficiently understood, we can then frame regulations by obedience to which dangers of infection may be reduced or in some cases eliminated. Medical ordinances are thus based upon knowledge of the laws of pathology —one of the divisions of " natural law "; by voluntary obedience to these ordinances the health of the body may be preserved and the life of the individual prolonged. Our rules of health follow in the wake of our understanding of its laws; the laws are themselves self-acting, and not subject to our control; the rules are ordinances which we may follow or neglect as we please. So also the spiritual life is lived under the government of law—law none the less natural because spiritual. In this sphere also certain results follow on certain actions. This line of conduct conduces to spiritual health, that line to spiritual disease and death. The spiritual life, no less than the natural, of which it is the highest stratum, must be nourished and preserved from adverse influences. In the bodily life we possess the instinct of self-preservation ; we instinctively put out our hand to avoid a blow, instinctively flinch from bodily pain, instinctively draw back from fore-seen danger. Nor is it otherwise with the spiritual life ; in it also we have the instinct of self-preservation. But as the spiritual life is deeper and more fundamental, so its dangers are less palpable and more complex. The spiritual instinct has to be a delicate instrument, sensitive to the approach of harmful influences such as tend to impair or destroy the spiritual vitality.

The spiritual life is not a figment of the imagination ; it is no less real, and more fundamental, than our bodily life ; if we call it "supernatural," we only mean that it is the highest manifestation of the natural. And the

self-preservative faculty for this higher, in-
tangible part of ourselves is called Conscience.
Conscience tells us, " This way lies life." It is
only a compelling force in so far as we de-
liberately choose that it shall be. To avoid or
neglect its warning is to court spiritual disaster.
The instinct weakens with disuse ; the defences
of the spiritual life dwindle, as its dangers
multiply. It is a natural law which tells us
that the result of sin is spiritual illness, and
that in the last resort, the wages of sin is death.

This is a law of our spiritual nature, and
on the basis of this law are laid down the
ordinances, Thou shalt do this, and, Thou shalt
not do that. The natural law that sin leads
to death is simply a fact ; it does not ask for
our obedience or disobedience ; it is self-acting.

Thus we perceive that the operation of
natural law, from its highest to its lowliest
sphere, is, as it were, a game of consequences.
The consequences in all cases are natural, con-
gruous, inexorable. The bridge which is con-
structed for a stress of fifty tons breaks down
under a hundred ; the human body constituted
to resist a given dose of virus, gives way under
a greater dose ; the man who partakes of moral

poison becomes a moral invalid, and is on the road to spiritual death. These are all simple facts ; nothing can alter them.

I have called these results consequences. Others call them by different names ; some call them punishments. The engineer is punished for his faulty calculations ; the invalid is punished for exposing himself to infection ; the wastrel is punished for his sin. But if you use the term punishment, be sure you know the meaning of the word.

The word punishment has a moral reference, and implies moral responsibility in its object. For this reason we could not say that the bridge (of my illustration) is punished for its weakness; for punishment the responsible engineer had to be introduced. Again, in case of the illness, we had to suppose that the victim had culpably exposed himself to infection. In all cases the use of the word punishment tends to obscure the fact that each of the disasters is a necessary sequence ; the processes are self-acting ; God's special intervention is needless ; the results are automatic, not apart from His will, but by His will.

By its self-acting quality, therefore, God's

method of dealing with moral failure differs
from what we customarily term "punishment,"
as inflicted by human authority. Our punishments, whether in the family or the state, are
arbitrary in character. With us it is a question
of judging very imperfectly, and often quite
wrongly, the heinousness of the moral offence,
and then selecting a penalty which we deem
suitable. Our sublime object is to make the
punishment fit the crime. It were better,
indeed, to make the punishment fit the criminal,
for we are punishing the person, and not his
actions; but then we cannot see the inside of
the criminal's mind, and we must judge him by
his overt actions. Our punishments, therefore,
are arbitrary and external; God's judgement is
self-acting and internal. Sin fulfils its own
punishment; justice is axiomatic. What then
is the mode of God's judgement and punishment? It takes effect as spiritual degeneracy
and alienation from God. And the final end of
such separation from God must be total death,
since God is the source and upholder of
all life.

Some, of course, will object that such a
process does not, or need not, involve pain

to the punished; vengeance in its popular significance has gone; the sinner is not made to smart. But God's object is not to inflict pain on the unrepentant sinner. Such revenge contains the elements of hatred and cruelty, which have no place in the nature of God. The doctrine of eternal torment of the damned— torment as useless as it is eternal—no longer carries weight, because nobody believes it. God does not smite the sinner from without; the process works from within. When the sinner awakens to the true significance of his situation, then he feels the pain; when his spiritual consciousness is roused from anaesthesia, then he feels the smart of his self-inflicted wounds; then, indeed, there is pain; this pain is of God's determination, and its action is restorative. God inflicts no pain without a moral purpose. If there is in a man's soul capacity for such pain, there is of necessity a corresponding capacity for reform. It is the pang of the prodigal's heart that drives the prodigal home to his Father.

This is, I believe, in the last resort, the object of all human punishment, arbitrary and imperfect though it be. When the mother

punishes her child, it is, or ought to be, with
a single eye to the child's restoration to goodness: otherwise it is mere senseless revenge.
In the case of criminal justice, the issue is
obscured, because it seeks not only to punish
the offender, but to deter others from the like
offence; even so, the object of criminal punishment is more and more regarded as restorative
rather than retributory. Yet between parent
and child, the issue is a more strictly personal
one; and it is from this relation that we may
obtain the closest picture of God's dealings with
ourselves. Now the parent's chastisement is
wholly directed towards awakening in the child
a sense of repentance for the wrong done. If
it fails of this, it has been absolutely useless.
So also is it with the Father in Heaven; we
cannot think of Him inflicting pain in mere
vindictive anger. Such retribution as falls on
the evildoer, falls on him for reclamation, not
retaliation. And such external retribution,
when it does come, comes through the natural
social tendency which was summarised by Jesus
himself when he taught that " with what
measure ye mete, it shall be measured to you
again"; or simply, People will behave to you

as you behave to them—a generalisation which, even from a utilitarian standpoint, commends the golden rule, "As ye would that men should do unto you, even so do unto them."

Now, though such external retribution tends to fulfil itself in human society, yet it is not the result of an automatic machinery. It is a social tendency, not a "natural law." The law, however, that sin leads to death, is self-acting. Quite apart from any penalties inflicted from without, every man carries within himself a perfect register of his own deeds; his present spiritual state is the complete result of his past; for better or for worse he is the product of his own work. He needs no external judgement.

I have attempted to show that God's system of distributive justice is self-acting; it is part of the self-acting Law of Nature; it has nothing arbitrary or artificial about it; it does not necessarily contain any element of castigation or pain; yet it fulfils the strictest canons of justice; and it is sufficient.

But, someone will say, what then of "Eternal punishment"? What of the worm that dieth not and the fire which is not quenched? My answer is that these figures used in the gospels have been falsely interpreted. There is an eternal fire, and there is an eternal punishment; but neither of them answers to popular thought.

In the nature of God there is an inherent antagonism against wrong-doing. It is an eternal antagonism, because it lives in the thought of God. It is fitly represented as an eternal fire. It burns up, always and certainly, whatever reaches it of an inflammable kind. "The chaff he will burn with fire unquenchable." The fire is eternal; the chaff is not. The chaff is burnt up in a moment; the fire goes on. The destruction of the chaff is permanent, and in this sense its fate is properly described as eternal. The picture of the eternal fire contains in it no suggestion of torture, but an assurance that nothing that is evil can live before the presence of God.

So far, then, we have been discussing the justice of God, as operating through the laws of cause and effect, which He has imposed on the world, both in the physical and spiritual spheres. The justice of God is eternal and unalterable; it is the fixed principle of our spiritual being; it is the law of Spiritual Gravity. But while this is, as far as it goes, a true account of the matter, it gives us only a kind of scientific view of the mode by which God's justice comes into operation; it introduces us to a cold self-acting machinery, instituted, doubtless, by God; but it fails to bring us into warm contact with God Himself; it is not religion.

Yet we shall have gained something, if, before we enter the confines of personal religion, we have learnt to think aright about the facts of our spiritual environment, the things which form the background and circumstance of our religious life; thus only can we escape from the confusion of thought whereby love appears to come into collision with law, punishment with forgiveness, mercy with justice. For love is not opposed to law, nor mercy to justice.

The fixed laws of cause and effect, then, of which we have spoken, whether in the spiritual or material realms, are, as it were, the garment in which God clothes Himself in His dealings with man; in that garment He stands before us half-revealed, but also half-concealed. Hitherto we have considered this garment alone; but within the garment there beats the Heart of God, and above there smiles a Face.

# CHAPTER V

WE now direct our thought to God as a living Being; transcendent indeed, yet not unintelligible; exercising the functions of thought and will in a manner which, though extending beyond, is yet in line with our understanding. His holiness stretches over our horizon, yet what we see of it, we comprehend; His antagonism to evil is greater than we can imagine, yet of the same nature as our imagining.

Antagonism to evil! What do we mean by evil? for the very word evil is used in different senses. A man may be bad, or an egg may be bad. Both imply a standard set up in our mind—one for the man, another, quite different, for the egg. An earthquake may be spoken of as evil, because of its unfortunate effects on its victims. But neither the egg nor the earthquake possesses any moral qualities ; and only moral evil finds antagonism in God.

What do we mean when we say that God is antagonistic to sin ? Do we mean that He is opposed to an abstraction ? God deals with persons, not with abstractions. We want to know what is His attitude to persons, for religion is a personal thing. It is commonly said—and there is no more misleading catchword—that God hates the sin, and loves the sinner. But moral evil has no existence apart from a moral agent. Sin has no·meaning independently of its author ; the moral value of a deed lies not in the deed itself, but in the person of the doer. If God is to hate anything or anybody, it must be the sinner ; for it is with the sinner that He has relations. Does God then love and hate the same person at the same time ? The paradox arises from the use of the term hatred, which denotes to our mind something inconsistent with our best conception of God ; the word is flavoured with human frailty ; it reeks of passion, cruelty, malevolence ; and these have no place in the divine nature. The word antagonism is uncoloured by these things, and may rightly express the Divine attitude to evil-doers. He loves all men, and yet is in antagonism to wicked men. A simple example from human relations will point my meaning. Suppose, reader, that you have a son who has lied or stolen. What will be your attitude towards your boy, so long as he maintains the lie or conceals the theft? You may say indeed, "I hate the lie, but love the liar," or "I hate the theft, but love the thief"; yet such expressions, though they mean something to yourself, are hardly calculated to illuminate others. We want to get at the psychology of the thing. Your heart may be surcharged with love for your son; normally the current of love flows from one to the other in full circulation; but now it is interrupted; his lying or stealing has altered the relations between you. By his action, you may say, the boy has cut himself off from your love; the change is on his side, not yours. But while you say this, you are conscious that not only is the boy's relation towards you altered, but your relation to him is altered too. The new situation is one of mutual antagonism. This is not a negation of mutual love, but an

interruption of its activity. The shadow of
his sin has fallen on both of you. As the love
is mutual, so the antagonism is mutual also.
Before relations can be restored there must be
an act of forgiveness on your part as well as
of penitence on his. Not only is he in antagonism to you, but you are in antagonism to
him. And this, though you each love the other
deep down in your hearts. So also, in my
belief, is the case with God. When a man sins,
he not only cuts himself off from the active
love of God, but he also brings upon himself
active antagonism from God's side. God loves
all men; but towards the unrepentant wrongdoer that love is inoperative; the antagonism
on man's part brings into action an antagonism
from the side of God; not a malevolent, but a
holy antagonism, by reason of which it is truly
said that "God is angry with the wicked every
day."

Our relations with God, whether in alienation or in forgiveness, involve a psychological
process. They cannot be understood in terms
of commerce or of the law-courts, but only in
psychological terms. God is a spirit; only by
our spiritual nature do we come into contact

with Him. Hence our conception of God must be, not anthropomorphic in the cruder sense, but anthropopsychic; and conversely, we must conceive of man as theopsychic, if he is capable of personal relations with God.

It follows, that if we are to understand the forgiveness of God, we must think of it along the lines of human forgiveness, and draw our conclusions as to the former from a careful survey of the latter.

Human forgiveness, then, is a spiritual process; we are familiar with it, and it is capable of analysis. When we speak of divine forgiveness, do we mean the same thing or something different? Surely the same; for here is our chief point of spiritual affinity with God. Yet from the speculation of earlier theology, one would imagine that between man and man forgiveness means one thing, but between God and man quite another. Man's forgiveness—in our higher understanding—is free, noble, unselfish, without money or price; is not God's the same?

The identity in kind between human and divine forgiveness lies at the root of the teaching of Jesus. Human forgiveness he regards, not as an analogy of the divine, but as an adequate picture of it, just as the ideal relation of human fatherhood is a fit representation of God's. " Our Father," he tells us to pray, " forgive us... as we forgive." "If ye forgive not...neither will your Father forgive you."

How does he describe the Father's attitude towards His lost children? In terms of the human father. The lost coin, the lost sheep, the lost son—these constitute an ascending series, by which we may rise from the analogy to the reality; from things wholly material to things wholly spiritual; from the finding of a coin to the recovery of a soul. It is clear that, according to Jesus, we may safely argue from human forgiveness to the divine. Along this road, if anywhere, we shall find light.

Let us follow it further. Once again, your son has lied. He persists in his lie, though you know it to be false. An antagonism has sprung up on both sides, so that mutual love ceases to be operative. What is required to heal the breach? Will a suitable punishment put things right? You may flog your boy and leave him unrepentant; things are worse than before; you have played your trump card, and lost.

Or, without any flogging, the boy may come penitent and unlock his heart to you—tell me, parent, will you say you cannot forgive till you have flogged? Nay, the door of your heart opens, for your love cannot resist the filial call. External punishment may, if judiciously administered, prove a salutary moral discipline; but it does not purchase the forgiveness. Forgiveness may come without punishment, or punishment without forgiveness; they are not complementary, nor does the one flow from the other. The only penalty which is necessary, which always descends, is the self-acting penalty; the boy's wrong action has so far lowered his spiritual vitality, and set back his spiritual life. If he is to recover, he must retrace his footsteps; and this recovery dates from the turning-point of repentance; the father's forgiveness nurses the delicate plant of penitence into the fulness of spiritual life. But artificial penalty is no part of the forgiveness; free forgiveness is independent of all such punishment. Forgiveness is an internal, psychic process; punishment is non-psychic and external.

Forgiveness means the re-establishment of

cordial relations between estranged persons; it is a two-sided proceeding, in which both parties must coöperate; the forgiving spirit must be present on one side, and the repentant spirit on the other; only by repentance can the offender become forgiveable; towards the forgiveable[1] forgiveness is an act of both mercy and justice.

Forgiveness is not the same as forgivingness. You may adopt and maintain a forgiving attitude towards your enemy, and yet forgiveness may be impossible; forgiveness, like any other gift, may be refused; the will to forgive must meet the will to be forgiven. Forgiveness implies psychological exchange; it is a mutual act. Forgivingness is not an act but an attitude; and it is ineffectual until met by a responsive attitude on the other side.

We have arrived, then, at a point from which we see human forgiveness as a free spiritual process, whereby alienated persons again become reconciled and reunited. It is independent of anything in the way of artificial or arbitrary penalty.

Are we prepared to transfer this conception

[1] See Moberly, *Atonement and Personality*, p. 56.

in its entirety to the divine forgiveness? Is
our thought so in harmony with the divine
that we can safely postulate this *and nothing
more* as the principle of God's forgiveness? Is
not our concept of forgiveness fogged by a sense
of our own sinfulness, and spoilt by our failure
to plumb the depth of God's antagonism to sin?
Is not the whole thing anthropomorphic?

First, the anthropomorphism. We are anthropomorphic—or anthropopsychic as I prefer
to say—when we conceive of God in terms of
our human selves, our human thoughts, our
human relations. What else can we do? Our
only alternative is to say that God is not only
unknowable, but unthinkable; to think at
all, either of God or nature, implies anthropomorphism; for we can only conceive of that
which is without in terms of that which is
within. Anthropomorphism may be, and often
has been, crude; but it is purged when we
grasp that God is Spirit[1]. If man can grow
like God, then God must be like the best in
man. If man can be theopsychic, then God
must be anthropopsychic. To deny it is to deny

[1] See W. Scott Palmer, *An Agnostic's Progress*, p. 123 ff. The
book is pleasant reading and highly suggestive throughout.

any possible point of contact between God and man;—is in effect not agnosticism but atheism. So far as we are concerned, there is no God, if we are necessarily lacking in points of possible contact with Him. It is a necessity of our nature to conceive of God in the terms of our human spirit; we can do no other. Do we conceive of God as powerful? Anthropomorphic. As just? Still anthropomorphic. As loving? It is anthropomorphism gone crazy.

Yet Jesus was the most anthropomorphic teacher that ever lived. How does God love? As the father loves the prodigal son. How does God forgive? "Forgive us as we forgive." Nor is this merely a loose analogy, or a vague similitude; in Jesus's teaching human forgiveness is not only a similitude, but a condition of the divine; "for if ye forgive not...neither will your Father forgive you." The very word Father is saturated with anthropomorphism; yet the fatherhood of God is the unalterable basis of Christian thought. By the divine spirit alone (so thinks St Paul) can we cry "Father." So strong is his grasp of this central fact, that he inverts the history of thought, and finds that God's fatherhood is the archetype—He is the Father, from whom all fatherhood in heaven and earth is named.

Granted, however, that the principle of forgiveness is the same in God and man ; it may, nevertheless, be urged that God's perfection introduces an incalculable element when it comes into touch with man's imperfection. God may require more from man, before He can forgive, than man requires from his fellow-man. It may be our own sinfulness which bars us from demanding full expiation. " Forbear to judge, for we are sinners all." May it not be impossible for the Sinless One to forgive, as we forgive, without penalty ? This also, I think, is ruled out by the teaching of Jesus. According to him the kingdom of heaven is a kingdom of free forgiveness. The debtor servant, of the parable, was freely forgiven, and this very fact bound him freely to forgive his fellow-servant. God's free forgiveness is for Jesus the archetype of human forgiveness. The higher we go in the scale of human goodness, the fuller we find the exercise of free forgiveness ; the holier the man, the readier is his forgiveness, and the remoter any thought of penal infliction. Human forgiveness may be imperfect, but it is on the right lines; where it is most free, there it is most perfect.

Again, you may urge, human repentance is imperfect. It is good enough for our fellow-men, but not good enough for God. He must have some guarantee of the depth and value of our repentance. To this I answer, once again, it is disallowed by the teaching of Jesus. His disciples asked, "Are we to go on forgiving, time after time, when the offence is repeated again and again?" "Certainly," said Christ, "go on indefinitely." There, surely, no guarantee of good conduct is implied. Rather is forgiveness looked on as the fount and origin of future well-doing; it is the spiritual basis of an amended life; it is the prop of failure, the source of success. And yet the idea that God requires some guarantee of our future good conduct, before He can forgive, holds prominence to-day; Christ, by a new hypothesis, is portrayed as the guarantor, or guarantee, to God of our future conduct. And so, by a different route, we are dragged back into the law-courts and the endless welter of transactional hypothesis; for by this theory, too, God requires from man a guarantee which, in the nature of the case, man cannot provide. A similar criticism, in my judgement, is incurred by those who, while ostensibly rejecting any idea of a penal substitution, seek to replace it by what they term a representative penitence; the suggestion being that Christ, unifying himself with the whole human race, and taking them, as it were, under his wing, offered to God a perfect penitence for all. This manner of thought, the chief exponents of which have been McLeod Campbell and Moberly, is not only nebulous in itself, but it rests upon an insecure foundation. How can Christ offer any penitence at all? Penitence is the sorrow felt by the wrongdoer for his offence; repentance is a personal forsaking of sin, and a re-direction of life and will; for Jesus neither of these was possible. No one can repent of sins not his own, or experience penitence for the sins of others. Moberly, I know, thinks otherwise; he takes the matter even further; he says that *only* the perfect man can perfectly repent; that for one who has sinned perfect repentance is impossible, just because he has sinned and thereby damaged his spiritual powers[1]. This

---

[1] R. C. Moberly, *Atonement and Personality*, pp. 117 ff. and

is sheer paradox, and to me, I confess, conveys no meaning. It is as if he should say, "No man who has had enteric fever can perfectly recover, because his bodily tissues have been injured by the complaint ; the only person who can perfectly recover is the man who has never had the disease " ; which is nonsense. But even if it had any meaning, it could only lead us back into the region of satisfaction-hypotheses ; for here too, God requires a penitence which man, in the nature of the case, cannot offer.

That this form of satisfaction-theory is less crude than the earlier attempts we may freely

Ch. vi. throughout. The same attitude is taken up by W. H. Moberly in Essay vi. of *Foundations*, pp. 307, 308, where he states quite clearly the objections to his own view, but appears not to feel their force ; he brushes them aside in a short rhetorical passage. To both authors the thought of vicarious penitence seems essential ; objections to it are merely trifling with words. "If vicarious penitence is unmeaning and impossible, the problem of atonement is insoluble" (*Foundations*, p. 308) ; "If the perfection of atoning penitence cannot be achieved by the personally sinless, it will become...manifest that it cannot be either achieved or even conceived at all" (*Atonement and Personality*, p. 117). But in truth there is no need for pessimism. What is really in danger is not *any* theory of atonement, but the theory of atonement *by satisfaction*. All satisfaction-theories have a common weakness ; vicarious penitence is but a more dainty variant of vicarious penalty.

admit ; but it equally insists that God cannot forgive man apart from some satisfaction beyond man's power ; and this, I maintain, is neither to be found in the teaching of Jesus, nor to be deduced from it ; rather is it in flat contradiction of both his words and his actions.

Every explanation which is founded on satisfaction rendered to God by Christ, seems to draw a sharp distinction between the immediate aims of Christ and of God. This, to my mind, finds no justification in the New Testament. It is true that Christ is usually represented as the Saviour, and God as having sent him to perform that function. Yet God the Father is also represented, not once or twice but often, as Himself the Saviour. The phrase "God our Saviour" occurs no less than six times in the Pastoral Epistles ; St Luke uses the words "God my Saviour" ; in the Acts, St Paul is represented as speaking of "the Church of God, which He purchased with His own (Son's[1]) blood." Here it is God who purchases, God who saves ; and this I think is the

---

[1] It is difficult not to accept Hort's brilliant suggestion as to the original text of this passage. See Westcott and Hort's *Introduction to N.T.*, Appendix, p. 99.

mature conception both of St Paul and St John.
Such evidence is subversive of any suggestion
that Christ in any sense purchased our salvation
*from God.*   The action of Christ is rather
thought of as an expression of the Father's love,
winning men back to Himself by the revelation
of that which is within His heart.

How hard it is to read the gospels without
prejudice !   How hard to rid our minds of a
preconceived idea !   The free forgiveness of sins
was the vital spark of Christ's teaching.   " Thy
sins be forgiven thee."   Wherever he found
repentance, there he scattered forgiveness ;  it
was as water to the tender plant.   But it was
new doctrine, and very hard to receive ; fitting
so pat and glove-like to the measure of man's
need, it was surely too good to be true.   And
so this central teaching became overlaid, obscured, and contradicted ;  the very acts of
forgiveness by Christ, during his ministry,
became interpreted as an advance-benefit of
his own death—a purely fanciful contrivance,
admirably invented to bolster up a common
prejudice ; of such a thing there is no sign in
the forgiving words of Jesus, and there could be
no understanding in the mind of the recipient.

The doctrine of free forgiveness permeates both the teaching and the practice of Jesus. It is a corollary of the doctrine that God is love. But it is constantly suppressed as incompatible with God's justice ; justice, it is assumed, is not satisfied unless God should get His pound of flesh. Yet if you think of forgiveness simply in its personal relation, free forgiveness is a perfectly reasonable thing. When a man repents and turns away from his sin, he is, by that very fact, forgiveable ; the forgiveness of such an one is an act of righteousness as well as of mercy, for in respect of his fault the man *is* righteous ; God forgives the repentant, not in spite of justice, but because of justice. God's attitude to men is not that of justice tempered with mercy : not the resultant of a collision of two opposing forces : not a compromise between two contrary tendencies within the nature of God. Mercy and justice are met together, not in collision, but in harmony ; all the forces within the divine nature are operating in the same direction—that of forgiveness. To forgive the unrepentant is impossible ; not to forgive the repentant is equally so.

To some it will seem that the doctrine of free forgiveness is in flat contradiction of the thesis of my earlier pages. "There," I shall be told, "you made out that every evil act sets its indelible mark on the doer, and that he cannot escape the consequence; now you say that as soon as he repents, he is certain of immediate forgiveness with God." The two things are complementary truths, not contradictory. An ass or an ox may fall into a pit; but that does not prevent it from scrambling out again if it can, or being pulled out, if it cannot. The laws of nature are not contravened by either operation. Or take another example. If I sustain a severe wound, or fracture my arm, the knowledge that nature must take her course does not prevent the surgeon from dressing the wound or setting the fracture in a favourable position. Nature has her way in either case; but the results are very different. In the one case the wound will suppurate and the fracture will not unite; in the other the bone will knit, and the wound will heal, leaving only a scar to register the past. The surgeon has but directed the course of nature; he has skilfully guided the vital

forces to compass recovery. He has not contravened nature's laws; he has understood
them. The constant operation of the laws of
action and reaction gives the condition to all
our activities, and their understanding is the
basis of all our progress. Just as the processes
of natural life form the constant background of
the surgeon's activity, so the process of action
and reaction in the spiritual sphere forms the
background of all mutual personal activity,
whether of man towards man, or of God towards man. So when God forgives the sinner,
His action in no way contravenes the law that
sin leads to spiritual death, any more than you
interfere with the law of gravity when you pull
your beast out of a hole. Forgiveness is the
restoration of the sinner to the path of life, and
is based upon the assumption that sin is the
way of death. And this comprehensive view
of the matter is summarised in the words: "The
wages of sin is death, but the gift of God is
everlasting life." The law of man's nature
has not ceased to operate, but a new force
has entered the scene—the force of personal
inspiration.

God's forgiveness then is free; it is not

obtained by transactions, satisfactions or guarantees beyond our ken; it is only conditioned by repentance; this condition is not one arbitrarily imposed, but inherent in the proposition; repentance alone is receptive of forgiveness; acceptance is the condition of all giving.

If, then, God is always ready to forgive in response to repentance, it would at first sight appear as if the only activity to be evoked is an activity on man's part. He has, as it were, only to come and drink of a fountain which is always flowing, to partake of a feast which is always prepared, to put (may we suggest it?) his spiritual penny into the spiritual slot. Yet these metaphors are all illusory, if pressed. The proceeding is a personal one; God is not a fountain, or a feast, or an automatic machine. It is precisely here that we are apt to be misled. One well-known author[1] has suggested that God's forgiveness is self-acting; if this is so, then the metaphor of the automatic machine is not hyperbolic. The laws, by which the universe is ordered, are self-acting, and are properly called so; but the personal relationships

[1] Moberly, *Atonement and Personality*, pp. 57, 58.

of God are not self-acting ; with God, as with
men, forgiveness is an act of self-revelation,
an opening of His heart to His creatures, an
active giving.   True, the more God-like the
human father, the more certain is the prodigal
son of forgiveness, when he comes repentant.
But is the forgiveness therefore self-acting ?
Verily no.   Because you can always be sure
of the generous conduct of a friend, do you call
his generosity automatic ?   Because you trust
a man implicitly, is his faithfulness self-acting ?
Theirs is not the dead consistency of auto-
matism, but the living constancy of spiritual
strength.

The distinction is a vital one.   Reconciliation
involves giving as well as taking; it is a doubly-
active spiritual process.   Read the story of the
prodigal's return, and you will see.   The father's
activity dominates the picture with his im-
pulsive love.   " While he was yet a great way
off, his father saw him, and had compassion, and
ran and fell on his neck, and kissed him."   His
love leaps forth to meet the approaching penitent ; it is all alive ; it embraces, forgives,
restores, protects.   If the son's return is a thing
of action, even more so is the father's welcome.

Not without a doubly-active mutual embrace is the work of restoration completed; only so can love again become operative.

But are the relations just as before? Is the father's love the same as before the son went away? No; something has been added; the quality of the thing is different; before, it had the diamond's brightness: now it has a richer ruby glow. Before, there was love in the father's eye; but now it shines through a tear. In that tear lies hid the mystery of forgiveness.

# CHAPTER VI

I HAVE insisted that God's forgiveness is free to the repentant sinner; but I have also suggested that there is something in the heart of God in relation to that forgiveness, which we have not yet fathomed. I now propose to look for the evidence and explanation of that something in the life of Jesus; to inquire how his life and death are related to the forgiveness of sins.

Jesus certainly had a clear conception of his mission, and of the significance of his own life. His own account of it was not dependent on the circumstances or manner of his birth. His claims were to be judged on the merits of his life. He claimed to bring men a revelation of God; to teach them the truth about God; that God was their Father, that God was love. But more than this, and transcending this, he

claimed himself to *be* a revelation of God.   His
works, his words, his thoughts,—the whole
attitude and outlook of his life, were of the
divine quality.   He is the way to God; he
is the truth of God; he is the divine life.
When his disciples besought him to shew them
the Father, the answer came, " He that hath
seen me hath seen the Father."   So it appears
that if we wish to know about the activities
of the Father, we are directed to look at Jesus.
The object of his mission, as he conceived it,
was not to conduct transactions with the Father,
but to reveal the Father to men.   His love
was the Father's love; his forgiveness was the
Father's forgiveness...and what shall we say of
his sufferings ?

The meaning of this element in his life was
clear enough to his own mind.   In order to
fulfil his revelation of the Father, he must
needs suffer.   This his disciples could not
understand; and his disciples of later times,
while they have accepted the fact, have failed
also to understand it.   All sorts of reasons have
been given why the Christ must needs suffer,
except the true reason.

"Father, forgive them."   Why does the

spirit of forgiveness, which radiates from the cross of Jesus, count for so much in the world? Because it cost much. It is the cost of forgiveness with which we have to do, when we face the problem of Atonement.

Forgiveness which does not involve cost is not worth the name. Formal pardon for an offence which does not hurt, has no moral value. But the father's pardon of his returning prodigal has value, because it represents love which has lived through pain. Herein alone lies the value of pardon. The worth of forgiveness is measured exactly by the intensity of the suffering inflicted by the offender. That is the cost of forgiveness; and in the nature of the case, it is a cost borne by the injured person, and not by the wrongdoer.

The point is of ultimate importance. You may say that the wrongdoer ought to bear the brunt of his own evil deed; but the whole meaning of forgiveness is that he does not, and that the other does. It is not a substitution, but an infliction; not a flimsy hypothesis, but a hard fact. He who forgives, has borne the smart inflicted without retaliating; his love has lived through pain; the plant of love, in the garden of his heart, saved from the killing bite of frost, tended with care and sunned from heaven, has thrown a blossom of forgiveness; its beauty and fragrance are for the other, having plucked it, to enjoy. But that flower does not grow wild; it needs much labour, and is very costly.

Does not this kind of costliness enter into divine as well as human forgiveness? Is it not with such a thought that we should study the life of Jesus?

Now if we turn to the New Testament, we shall find in the minds of all the writers a conviction that there is some vital relationship between the sufferings of Jesus and the forgiveness of sins. "This is my blood, which is given...for the forgiveness of sins." "My blood which I will give for the life of the world." Not only do we find it in the Gospels; it pervades the Apostolic teaching in the Acts; it echoes through the epistles, not only of St Paul, but also St John, St Peter, and the writer to Hebrews[1]. And from that time

[1] *E.g.* from St Paul, "In whom we have redemption through his blood, even the forgiveness of sins," Eph. i. 7: St Peter, "Ye were redeemed by the precious blood of Christ," 1 Pet. i. 19:

to this, it has been a constant part of the Christian faith, that somehow, through the passion of Christ, we obtain the forgiveness of sins. The close relationship of these two ideas has been elaborated by several modern authors, and I think they have justified their contention. Too often, however, they have made it a foundation on which they build a theory of satisfaction by substitution; and with such a conclusion I have no particle of sympathy. The matter in which I differ from such writers, and differ profoundly, is that with them the process is transactional, legal, imputative, artificial; for me the process is inherent and vital.

Let us try to divest our minds of preconceptions, and strive to appreciate the meaning of Christ's passion in its historical setting. Jesus was wickedly put to death by wicked men; he bore their sin, not in the conventional, supramundane sense, but really and actually; not a penalty, but a direct infliction. This

St John, "The blood of Jesus Christ cleanseth us from all sin," 1 John i. 7 : Heb., "To put away sin by the sacrifice of himself," Heb. ix. 26 : Acts, "Through this man is preached unto you the forgiveness of sins," Acts xiii. 38.

infliction he bore to the end, and to the end
the light of forgiving love shone from his eye.
The process was the same as the process of all
human forgiveness ; its value is measured by
suffering. It is the very intensity of the sufferings of Jesus which lends supreme significance
to the cry "Father, forgive them." That forgiveness was surely divine ; yet by its intensity
only is it marked off from that which we call
human ; for in fact the process of all forgiveness
is the same ; and all is divine.

Again and again we find in Christ's utterances this same trend of thought—the costliness
of forgiveness. The sheep which has gone
astray is recovered by the labour and at the
cost of the shepherd ; the servant is forgiven
his debt—at the expense of his lord. But in
the story of the lost son we have the climax ;
for here we have no analogy, but the real thing :
by a divine alchemy, love has found an antidote
for the poison ; the very reckless injury to the
father's heart has evoked from that heart, not
the bitterness of revenge, but the joyful welcome
of forgiving love—joyful through tears. So we
may find in Jesus's teaching, as well as in his life,
that forgiveness to his mind was a thing of cost.

Not only, however, is there, in the nature of things, an intimate and vital connexion between forgiveness and suffering, but suffering is a necessary antecedent of forgiveness. The two processes do not run, as it were, on parallel lines, but the one flows from the other; forgiveness is sequential to suffering, and suffering alone can render forgiveness possible. Forgiveness is the end, suffering is the means. *Without suffering there is no forgiveness.* Thus we arrive, by a different route, it is true, at a similar conclusion as the New Testament author, when he found the same principle underlying both Hebrew and Christian thought,—the principle that "without shedding of blood there is no remission." It were too much to set about to prove that the thought of this necessary psychological relation of suffering to forgiveness lay implicit in the whole sacrificial system of Hebrew antiquity; yet such an idea could not be condemned as preposterous[1]. The need for divine forgiveness and the longing to participate in the divine life are fundamental to religious thought in all ages; the slain lamb represented

[1] It seems consistent with the facts advanced by Robertson-Smith, *Religion of the Semites.* See specially Lect. VIII., pp. 287 ff.

to the mind of the Semites the divine life of which they were to partake. But whether or no we regard the ancient ritual of sacrifice as founded on a true spiritual instinct, yet it is clear that Christ and his disciples took these dry bones of sacrificial ritual, clothed them in flesh and blood, and breathed into them a new and throbbing vitality.

The necessity of suffering as antecedent to forgiveness—the δεῖ παθεῖν—this is the dominant note of Christ's ministry; it underlies the whole tragic history; it forms the constant recurring theme, and harmonises at every point with his words and works. He who would forgive must needs suffer.

In this, if in aught else, Christ was the revelation of God. He was doing the things which he saw the Father doing : in him the Father stood revealed. Is the Son afflicted by the wickedness of men ? So is the Father. Does the Son suffer by reason of sin ? So does the Father. Does the Son suffer lovingly, willingly, always in the spirit of forgiveness, made perfect through suffering ? So does the Father. It is no new doctrine, that the Son, in suffering, declares the Father to us ; his life and death alike were the exhibition of God's love for the human race. The lesson of the cross is the lesson that God loves the world. Why, it is the message of the Gospel. There is no other.

When love comes in contact with moral evil, when the loving God comes into touch with the sinner, then if that love is to result in reconciliation and forgiveness, suffering must be the means and method. It is certainly true in men; Jesus came to tell us that it is true in God.

Can Almighty God suffer? Is not God impassible? If God is passible, if He can suffer, does not this bring Him down from His supreme pedestal of omnipotence, of unchangeableness, of eternal bliss? The answer is short: God is love. We must take God down off any pedestal on which love cannot stand. Such pedestals are of our own making. That God is a God of power and order and knowledge—this is true. But in relation to his spiritually-conscious creatures, all this is of minor importance; to us the crucial point is that He is love. Now love is passible; and if God is love, God is passible. A person who can love, and yet cannot suffer, is unimaginable; and if God is such, He is unthinkable; for we cannot think of a love that is out of range of suffering. Love and suffering dwell in one house. Nay, they are twin sisters; they live and grow together; hardly are they known apart, but that the dress of one is of a more sombre hue. If the love be great, great also is the power of suffering; and if God's love be infinite, then He can suffer infinitely too. The doctrine of the impassibility of God, taken in its wide sense, is the greatest heresy that ever smirched Christianity; it is not only · false, it is the antipodes of truth. It is the negation of Christ's message. By this door has entered false thought and false conception of every kind. That God Almighty can and does suffer in relation to His sinful creatures,—this is a cardinal doctrine of Christianity.

Do you think such love the negation of omnipotence? I answer boldly, No. A door of steel you may break with force; the door of man's heart cannot be forced; it has to be opened from the inside; against the will of free-willed man, force is no remedy; love is the only omnipotence.

But again you say, God is unchangeable. Yes, He is unchangeable; but His is not the unchangeableness of a stone. Of a true friend we say, He never changes. We do not mean that his expression does not change, or that he is always doing the same thing, still less that he never does anything at all. It is his will and purpose of friendliness which does not change. God's is not the inactive unchangeableness of a lifeless thing; His is the active changelessness of a living spirit; changelessness of will and purpose; and those are the will and purpose of love. The changelessness of God stands in contrast to the changefulness of man. Man's imperfect knowledge, the imperfect processes of his thought, drive him to change his mind, to retrace his footsteps, to alter his direction; he wastes his activities and misdirects his energies; God is constant in His purpose, uniform in His direction, unswerving in His will. In this sense God is changeless, and this is all the changelessness we need postulate of Him. Whatever of change is inseparable from life, action, and fulfilment of purpose, such change is not incompatible with Godhead.

Thus we find that passibility in God,

involving as it does love and suffering, need
not be regarded as a contradiction of that power
and stability which are necessary attributes of
the divine.   For love alone assures constancy
of purpose, and love alone can carry the citadel
of an estranged heart.

But before love can win, it must be perceived by its object; before forgiveness can
become operative with man, it must be made
manifest to his mind.   And this, I take it,
was the object and mission of Jesus; to shew
to man, projected, as it were, on to the screen
of human life, the hidden life of God; to unveil
to man's inward eye the face of God; to prove
to man that God's heart is a wounded heart,
yet a perfectly forgiving heart, because a heart
of inextinguishable love.

That God loves us; that He is wounded by
our wrong-doing; that these wounds cause Him
suffering; that only by and through the ordeal
of suffering can His heart produce for us the
gift of forgiveness; this is what Christ came to
teach.   And this, however it has been obscured
by defective explanation,—this, I say, has been
the fundamental instinct which has drawn men's
hearts up to God; the belief that on the cross

is seen a living picture of the love of God; that God is revealed in terms of the Christ; that " God is reigning from the tree."

I observe, however, that certain writers fight shy of pressing this doctrine of the passibility of God to its proper conclusion, on the ground that it savours of the heresy of Patripassianism[1]. The objection is based on a misunderstanding of what that heresy was. The Patripassians denied a personal distinction between the Son and the Father; Noëtus, their leader, taught that " the Father himself endured birth, suffering and death in the flesh." It was one of the phases of the Christological controversy, and really has no bearing on our present discussion. I do not, of course, for a moment suggest that God the Father suffered death here on the cross : I do maintain that as Jesus suffered on earth from man's sin, so God the Father suffers always in heaven. The distinction is so obvious, that I need not labour the matter further.

Indeed, I am not aware that the Christian church of any age has ever denied that God Almighty suffers in relation to sin. Such impassibility as has been formally recognized has

[1] *E.g.* Stevens, *Christian Doctrine of Salvation*, p. 218.

never gone further than a denial that God is subject to passions which might affect the justice of His actions and His orderly conduct of the universe; in this sense divine impassibility is generally admitted. The kind of passibility which results from the impact of sin on the heart of a loving God—this is of a different character.

While, however, the latter kind of passibility has never formally been denied, it must be admitted that it has not, until recent years, met with much encouragement. To fathers, schoolmen and reformers alike, it seemed a sort of impiety to attribute to God Almighty even the potentiality of pain or suffering. Even Anselm, perceiving the damage which God sustains from sin, expresses it in terms of violated honour—a cold, impersonal sensitiveness,—rather than the warm personal distress of a wounded heart. Such a passibility as this was probably beyond the range of the early or mediaeval theologians; it was not demanded by their theories, and they failed to see in it a necessary corollary to the Christian faith. To theologians of to-day it makes a stronger appeal. To-day it is felt that if we accept as

truth the transcendent personality of God—
and the Christian faith demands it—then we
cannot stop short of investing that personality
with such attributes as seem to us inseparable
from the ideal personal life. A personal God
who cannot love tenderly, nor suffer in relation
to that love, though better than an abstraction,
is little better than a statue ; when pricked
it does not bleed; when pleased it does not
smile ; an outstretched hand it does not grasp.
We do not want a monarch in his robes of
state, but a king whose home is in his people's
heart, and theirs in his. If we are to invest
God with personality at all, it must be alive
and warm ; if it can love, it must needs be
capable also of suffering.

So deeply is this felt to-day that it is
hardly possible to take up any modern book
on the subject where it does not find some
expression[1].

Fifty years ago it found early vent in the
work of Horace Bushnell : " There is a cross in

[1] Examples may be found in Stevens's *Christian Doctrine of Salvation*, pp. 391, 436, 481, Oxenham's *Catholic Doctrine of Atonement*, p. 341, W. Temple's *Faith and Modern Thought*, p. 135, Hinton's *Mystery of Pain*, p. 40, McDowall's *Evolution and the Need of Atonement*, pp. 148, 153.

God," he says, "before the wood is seen upon
Calvary, hid in God's own virtue itself[1]."
"This is the eternal story of which Christ
shows us but a single leaf[1]." And to-day in
*Foundations* we find quoted with approval an
echo of the same thought : "There was a cross
in the heart of God before there was one
planted on the green hill outside of Jerusalem.
And now that the cross of wood has been
taken down, the one in the heart of God
abides, and it will remain so long as there is
one sinful soul for whom to suffer[2]." This is
a mode of thought which needs no apology.
What is it but a rediscovery in our day of the
picture of "the lamb slain before the foundation
of the world" (Rev. xiii. 8), and of that vision
of the heavenly throne, in whose centre is seen,

---

[1] Bushnell, *Vicarious Sacrifice* (1866), p. 73 ; *Forgiveness and
Law* (1874), p. 60. The latter book I have read since this study
was mainly finished. The first chapter is a remarkable contribution, specially in view of its date (1874); I find in that chapter
(not in the rest of the book) numerous and important points of
contact with my own point of view; more so, I think, than in
any other single work. He does not entirely get away from the
satisfaction theories, but they are only retained as satisfactions
elaborated within the mind of God, and not as supplied *ab extra*.

[2] *Foundations*, p. 322, quoted from Dinsmore, *Atonement in
Literature and Life*.

not the trappings of royalty, but a wounded heart. (Rev. v. 6). I am persuaded that this represents a true and most fruitful tendency of modern thought. At first sight indeed there is a seeming incompatibility between almightiness and suffering, between God and pain, between supremacy and self-sacrifice ; but when we come to close quarters with that difficulty it does not really constitute a philosophic *impasse.*

Pain, indeed, simply inflicted from without, and answering to nothing within the being of the sufferer, does certainly suggest weakness and involuntary limitation. We could not, for instance, think of God as suffering from the tooth-ache ; but when the submission to pain is voluntary, with motive and object defined, then suffering acquires a dignity, for it lies on the road to achievement. On the one hand is limitation, on the other self-limitation.

Now any act on the part of God, even a creative act, involves Him in some sort of self-limitation. The doctrine of the *kenosis*—the self-emptying of God—is not a mere invention of Christian dogmatists, but a necessity of philosophic thought. Any act of self-expression involves a corresponding self-limitation. God may have an infinite potentiality of self-expression ; but having determined its direction, He is limited to travel along the line of His own choice. If He chooses the expansion of love, He thereby chooses the limitation of self-sacrifice, and even of suffering. He is not driven to it ; He chooses it : it is no derogation to His infinitude.

The late James Hinton, in his illuminating little book, *The Mystery of Pain*, points out that even in our human sphere, self-sacrifice on behalf of someone we love, need not be felt as pain. " Love when it is strong," he says, " can banish pain.... We are not only willing, we rejoice, to bear an ordinarily painful thing for the benefit or pleasure of one whom we intensely love " (*Mystery of Pain*, pp. 34, 35 ff.). Under such circumstances it is not felt as pain. The pain is latent if present at all ; it does not rise to the surface of consciousness ; it is insulated from our perception by the love which involves it. So, perhaps, in the perfection of God's love, there is no pain, but only joy, in His self-sacrifice.

Such a consideration is most helpful ; but

it does not carry us the whole way. The author himself feels (pp. 79, 80, 96, 97) that it is not an adequate account of the suffering inflicted on God by man's sin; the pain of contact with moral evil cannot thus be eliminated or made as if it were not; in face of sin, His holiness and love must bring about not a mitigation but an aggravation of suffering. "Was there ever sorrow like unto my sorrow?" Such distress could only be met in the strength of a great hope and a steadfast purpose; such pain could only be willingly borne in the certain confidence of the ultimate triumph of forgiving love. If the perfections of God make His self-sacrifice a joy, they also intensify His distress at the touch of unrighteousness. And each of these truths within the divine being is seen reflected in the historical crucifixion.

For God and for man alike the way of forgiveness must be the way of the Cross. But, in maintaining this as a fundamental truth, I do not wish to suggest that the act of forgiveness is in itself a painful thing to the soul that forgives. On the contrary, it is, or it ought to be, a joyful and happy function. But the power to perform that function is only attained at the cost of suffering. The act of forgiveness is an act of happy reunion ; so happy as to blot out the painful memory of its costliness. But this makes its costliness none the less real ; every soul that forgives has passed through its hour of distress.

Jesus, then, upon the cross, is to us the glory and the power of God ; for there he is a picture of the action, the suffering and the love of the Father whom he came to reveal. This is no heresy, but fundamental Christianity. Forgiveness is the crown of love ; so the love of Jesus had to be made perfect through suffering ; for without suffering there is no forgiveness. And in all this Jesus revealed God. He was showing us God's nature, property, character. As Christ was to those who wronged him, such is God to us ; as Jesus suffered from the wickedness of men, so God suffers too ; as Jesus had to suffer in order that he might forgive, so can God's forgiveness proceed only out of a wounded heart ; and as Christ was made perfect through suffering, so we may truly say that God's love, passing through suffering to forgiveness, seeks its proper crown, and works out its own inherent perfection.

# CHAPTER VII

## FORGIVENESS VITAL NOT FORMAL

I HAVE attempted to sketch in the last chapter an explanation of why the Christ must needs suffer. That explanation is rooted in the facts of human psychology, and is based on the actual process of human forgiveness. Now if this is to be our confession of faith, what becomes of the current controversies over this subject? It seems to me that those controversies disappear one by one; the point of view is altered; the distortions, which result from our visual medium, have vanished. What, for instance, becomes of the transactional theories? those processes which have been supposed to go on between the Father and the Son, those arrangements, agreements, compromises, plans? how the Son propitiated and appeased the Father, how Jesus's holiness, submission and suffering brought satisfaction to the offended righteousness, justice and majesty of his God ? Why, it all seems to me to vanish like a mist. Jesus forgave because Jesus suffered, and the Father forgives because the Father suffers. Neither would suffer if He did not love. God does not forgive because another suffers ; God must needs suffer Himself if He is to forgive. There is no transaction ; forgiveness is free to the repentant ; its cost has been paid by the heart that forgives.

From this point of view, also, I think, we shall find that we have lost sight of those controversies which concern the subjective and objective relations of the atonement. This atonement was supposed to consist of two parts : first, the effect which the suffering of Jesus has on the minds of men ; secondly, the effect which it had on the mind of God. This suggests that Christ's function as mediator is that of a third person, inducing two belligerents to come to terms under which neither party's honour suffers. But this is surely a travesty of Christianity ; not in this sense is Jesus a mediator. He mediated by bringing down God's love to the range of human ken, and drawing men up into intelligent contact with it. Such mediation was needful to bring God's love within men's reach, and to make it operative towards them; but the mediator did not create the love, he only revealed it. He was himself an expression of it, and no third party. Did Christ's death, then, produce no effect whatever on God? Had it no objective effect in producing a different attitude in God towards us, as it admittedly awakens in us a different attitude towards God? I answer, Absolutely none. God's attitude towards sinful men was revealed by Jesus; but it was not altered by anything which Jesus did or could do. It is always the same; it always has been; it always will be. God does not change.

But, I shall be told, surely Christ *did* something on the Cross. Was there not a *work* which he finished there? What did he mean when he said, "It is finished"? The answer is simple and perfectly clear. The work which he finished was to reveal the Father to men. It was to shew to mankind in his life, sufferings and death, the nature and character of God; to draw men to himself and through himself to God.

This conception of Christ's work is certainly that which is taken in the fourth gospel, from which the thought of a finished work is derived. In ch. xvii. (the prayer, we might call it, of filial unity) we find the sequence of thought : "I have glorified Thee...I have finished the work which Thou gavest me to do...I have manifested Thy name to the men whom Thou gavest me...they know that all things whatsoever Thou hast given me are from Thee." St John has no idea of any satisfaction or expiation rendered to God ; to his mind the finished work of Jesus was the completed manifestation of the Father. And that is conceived of as a work accomplished by his whole life, and finished only when that life was yielded up on the cross. Therefore, at least in respect of the "finished work" of Jesus, the fourth gospel seems pointedly to support my contention. I will even go further than this, and say that the whole conception of thought in the fourth gospel is one which fits well and closely with the synthesis of doctrine which I here seek to build up.

And while I claim that such a conception is in close accord with the religious philosophy of the fourth gospel, I do not feel that it clashes with the views of the author of the Epistle to the Hebrews, or with (at least) the later epistles of St Paul. I do not pretend that it is derived from any of these, but only that it does not come into collision with them. That it can hardly be squared with many of the expressions in the earlier epistles of St Paul, we may frankly admit. The earlier epistles—so dear to the old school of theology—represent St Paul's mind still struggling toward a Christian developement, not yet wholly freed from the trammels and moulds of his traditional Rabbinic thought; the later epistles, such as that to Ephesus, show us the matured mind, expressed in metaphors less startling indeed, but more illuminating, antitheses less abrupt but more profound. To learn a man, we must learn what he developed into, not only what he developed from.

And if the views here expressed find themselves in general harmony with the thought of the great Christian writers, they are in still better accord with what we know of the expressed thought of Jesus. I have already suggested instances of this, and beyond such examples I am content to leave the matter to

the reader's judgement.    Two instances—and
only two, I think—can be adduced as out of
harmony with such a view, and as favouring the
earlier conception.

The first of these is, "The son of man came
...to give his life a ransom for many." A ransom
(λύτρον), it is said, must be paid to somebody.
The earlier or patristic theology said that it
was paid to the devil; the later mediaeval and
earlier protestant divines claimed that it was
paid to God.    Each of these conclusions in
turn had to sit on the back of an overworked
metaphor; for the cost of redemption needs not
to be paid to anyone.    The forgiving, suffering
love of a wife may redeem her husband, or the
husband's his wife; the cost of reclaiming the
one falls on the other; yet who shall say to
whom the price is paid?    Every noble action is
a thing of cost; but by "cost" we only mean
the expenditure of spiritual energy towards a
noble purpose.    And the cost of our forgiveness
is that suffering within the heart of God, which
alone made it possible.

The second instance is the cry, "My God,
My God, why hast thou forsaken me?" I think
no passage in literature has been so distorted

from its true meaning. It is the supreme instance of the eternal " Why ? " of innocent
suffering. Its very existence is proof that the
heart still trusts in God, though it cannot see
the way. It is the cry of high faith calling out
of the thick darkness. It is the fearful ordeal
of the soul, wherein men are invited to doubt
not only the love, but the very existence of God.
But in the case of Jesus, the triumphant issue
was never for a moment in doubt.

The thing is of such high import that it
must be touched on more fully. In quoting the
psalm (xxii.) Jesus presumably meant what the
psalmist meant. Now it is abundantly clear
that the psalmist did *not* mean that God had
in fact deserted or forsaken the sufferer. The
sense is defined in the second clause, " Why art
thou so far from helping me ? " forcing us to
interpret the first : " Why has God *left* me to
suffer thus ? Why does He not intervene?" But
such a sense of the Father's non-intervention,
combined with a feeling of utter loneliness—
desolation, if you like—this is a different thing
entirely from a loss of trust, confidence and
love. It has nothing to do with a sense of
spiritual separation, much less with a sense of

the Father's wrath. It has its counterpart in
the feelings of a son in affliction and distress,
away from the protection of his father's arm;
lonely indeed, yet never for a moment doubting
the father's love, compassion, and sympathy.
Later in the psalm we read: "He hath not
despised nor abhorred the affliction of the
afflicted, neither hath he hid his face from
him; but when he cried unto him he heard."
Precisely; it was the cry of faith groping
in darkness, soon to emerge into the light
of joyful understanding.

Such is the view rightly taken by McLeod
Campbell, Stevens, and other writers[1]. Not so
Dr Moberly, who finds its psychology and
exegesis alike defective. "It is assumed," he
says, "that the meaning of the words as used
by the psalmist is a measure of their meaning
in the supreme moment of the sacrifice of the
Crucified[2]." But what other exegetical basis
than this can we have, unless it be a basis of
theological preconception? What other clue
to Christ's meaning have we but the meaning

[1] Bushnell is of the same view; *Forgiveness and Law*, pp. 161,
162.

[2] R. C. Moberly, *Atonement and Personality*, p. 408.

of the psalm? Dr Campbell claims for Jesus
an unbroken trust in God, even in the hour of
his darkest extremity; Moberly rejects this
claim; and in his view, if I read him aright,
we are left to suppose that the trust of Jesus
in God did break down at the crisis; and this
for the very good reason that God had at that
crisis turned his face away and (for the time
being) had forfeited all claim to trust, confidence and love. That is not a pleasant picture
to contemplate; it is every bit as repellent as
the extremest doctrine of Calvinism, which the
same author energetically repudiates. The conception, in short, which is generally known as
the " Dereliction " on the cross, is a pure myth.
A real separation, even for a moment—not to
speak of separation in anger—between Jesus
and his God (if we regard him as human), or
between Son and Father (if we regard him as
divine) is as revolting to our spiritual instinct
as it is to our theology; it depends upon a
distortion of words which in their own context
have a plain and natural significance. It nega-
tives the note of perfect harmony with God
which forms the key-note of the life of Jesus;
at its beginning, " This is my beloved son, in

whom I am well-pleased"; in the middle, "He that sent me is with me; he hath not left me alone; for I do always the things that please him"; and at the end, "Ye shall all...leave me alone; and yet I am not alone because the Father is with me"; and again, "Therefore doth my Father love me because I lay down my life." Thus all considerations combine to forbid us to build on Psalm xxii. any edifice whatever of satisfaction or expiation paid by Jesus to God. The cry from the cross, while it transcended in degree, yet was the same in kind as the cry which is ever wrung from the heart of mankind in the extremity of suffering.

The explanation of the sufferings of Christ which I here attempt to bring forward is utterly different from any scheme of satisfaction rendered to God, whether by vicarious penalty or by vicarious penitence. My starting-point is that forgiveness involves suffering in the nature of the case—suffering which falls, not on him who is forgiven, but on him who forgives. Thus only can we find an interpretation which does not clash with the instincts both of reason and religion.

I fear that the course of the argument has led me into a large amount of negative criticism ; but I trust it has not been unfruitful of positive conclusion. Let me now pick up the threads of thought which have emerged in the foregoing chapters, and attempt to focus the mental picture.

God, our creator and preserver, has placed us in a world where certain laws of cause and effect have universal validity, and where our every action has its necessary result, not only on our surroundings, but on ourselves. Our physical developement, and equally our moral developement, is the outcome of our actions and habits in each particular sphere ; we deteriorate or improve according to fixed and self-acting laws; and in each case we are gifted with an instinct of self-preservation. Through our moral nature, thus conditioned and regulated, we have spiritual affinities, and a capacity of contact with the divine. God himself, being a spirit of love and holiness, while He loves everything He has made, yet is supremely sensitive to wrong-doing in His creatures. Therefore every evil action of men is not only, in the nature of the case, to their own detriment, but also is, as it were, a javelin aimed at the heart of God. Each wicked deed is not to be regarded as an affront to God, in consequence of which God, so to speak, turns away and sulks until He obtains satisfaction; it is rather a stroke aimed at the heart of God, *which gets home every time.* He is a suffering God because a loving God. Through suffering love alone comes the possibility of forgiveness. And this is true from all time : it is in the nature of God. It was not brought about by the advent of Jesus; Jesus was the expression of a love which, like all love, could not remain in willing silence; his life and his death were its continuous impersonation, showing the love which suffered and forgave : the love which (in a literal sense) bare the sin of many, and made intercession for the transgressors. And with the interceding words, " Father, forgive them," the forgiving spirit of Jesus fared back to the heart of God where it had been cradled.

The suffering of Jesus represented, not what man *ought* to suffer in expiation of his sin, but what God *does* suffer as a direct result of it, and having suffered is ready to forgive. This gives its sublime value to the forgiveness, which is expressed in the term "precious blood." In the suffering forgiveness of Jesus we see portrayed the suffering forgiveness of God.

Though God's attitude toward wrongdoing in men has always been the same, yet it was an attitude which had to be made apparent to men's thought.

The conception of God's fatherhood was not, indeed, totally new; yet it was supremely necessary to bring it home to men's minds, not as a theoretic analogy, but as a psychological reality. The true filial attitude can only be evoked by the perceived actuality of a Father's love. To this end some form of self-expression was required, which should exhibit God's love passing through suffering to forgiveness; and this could hardly be exhibited except by means of a perfect human life; for thus alone could love, suffering and forgiveness be shown in their true sequential relations. It has been already pointed out that suffering is a necessary antecedent to forgiveness; that without suffering true forgiveness cannot exist. But it is also true that love is the necessary antecedent of such suffering; for a certain kind of suffering —and that the deepest—is only made possible

by love. Not all suffering is of this kind;
I only speak of such suffering as is felt to have
its roots in personal relationship; the intensity
of such suffering must vary with the intimacy
of the personal bond. If a stranger injures
you, you may suffer physically or financially;
but if your friend injures you, there is a something added which strikes deeper and nearer
your heart; if it be your son who has wronged
you, this deeper, more spiritual element in the
suffering looms larger, and quite over-shadows
the physical or financial damage. Because, and
in proportion as, love enters in, you are liable
to this spiritual suffering; it is rooted in and
grows out of the love which precedes it. As
with us, so is it with God. Only because God
loves us does He come at all within the reach
of our injurious weapons; His love seeks re-
quital, and coming within our contact takes the
risk of rebuff. Because He loves us, therefore
we can injure Him; because He loves and is
injured, therefore He can forgive; the forgiveness is the compounded product of love and
suffering—not only their product but their
measure too.

By this line of reasoning it becomes clear

that suffering on the part of God, and therefore of Christ His revealer, is a necessary antecedent of divine forgiveness. But that necessity is derived from the nature of the case, and so far from needing any forensic or legal explanation, is totally inconsistent with it.

A vital religion cannot be cooped up in the cage of formal and outworn definition. The two sets of ideas, the formal and the vital, cannot live together; they are mutually exclusive. The older view, that of substitution, expiation, satisfaction, postulates a "give and take" in some form or other, between Jesus and God; these two are driving a bargain; mutually satisfactory, it may be, but still a bargain; they are looking at the thing from opposite points of view; the two persons of the Godhead are facing each other, reacting on each other, instead of both together facing and reacting on the wills of their erring creatures. The newer view which I have tried to lay before you, gives no action and reaction between Jesus and God, no bargain struck, no different point of view. The older hypotheses bristle with difficulties, moral and intellectual, which have made belief in them impossible to thoughtful men ; the newer view, *if once we can believe in a possible God*, is moral, spiritual, self-consistent.

The older conception is shattered on the rocks of thought. The questionings which it arouses are unanswerable. If God only forgives where the due expiation, already paid for sin, demands it, where do love and mercy come in ? If God is holy, how can He permit a system of vicarious penalty, which is, in our own sense of justice, both immoral and unjust ? If God's justice were (prior to the death of Christ) a bar to the exercise of His love, how should He send His Son at all ? Did Jesus first proclaim God's pardoning love, and then purchase it ? In this way, any theory of the atonement, in which Jesus expiates man's sin, drives us to postulate within the divine nature divergence and opposition, if not antagonism and contradiction. It is an edifice of the imagination which falls by its own weight.

The newer conception is entirely free from these antinomies ; it is based, not on hypothetical transactions of a supramundane sort, but upon that which is best and truest in human nature, coupled with a faith that those things which we know as best within ourselves have their counterpart—nay, their archetype—in God. This view demands, indeed, the belief that God can suffer; that He is passible; that He is affected by human action; that He can rejoice; that He can sorrow; that He can love. But this is the message of the Gospel—that God does love the world; and, loving, He must do and suffer all the rest. For us, who thus believe, Jesus is the representation and manifestation of God; in him we see the loving, the suffering, the forgiving, the rejoicing God; and with eyes resting on the crucifix, we lift our hearts to the God of self-expressive love.

The parable of the lost son gives us the key to the whole matter; it tells of a God who loves, suffers, forgives, and welcomes back to love. To believe in a personal God who loves, this is Christianity; to believe that God freely forgives the repentant and returning son, and that too at vast cost to Himself, this is Christianity as I conceive it; it is the burden of Christ's message; it is his living interpretation of God. The image which Jesus wished us always to have in our hands and before our eyes —the broken body, the shed blood—these are to bring repeatedly to our minds that God's forgiveness is a thing of cost.

The costliness is exemplified and brought home to us by the sufferings of Christ. In them, as in his whole life, we see, projected into the sphere of time, the eternal operations of the divine mind. They represent to us, not, as Grotius would have it, an armed demonstration to men of the Rights of God, but an unarmed, unresisting—albeit resistless—demonstration of the Love of God. The sufferings of Christ were directly due to the wrongdoing of the men of his own time, not of ours or of any subsequent age; yet to his disciples, both of his own and other ages, Jesus has revealed, once for all, the forgiving love of God. In this sense, the forgiving love of Jesus on the cross, though directed then towards those who wronged him, is still the medium through which God's forgiveness reaches men now; only by means of what Jesus did then upon earth, do we perceive what God is doing continually in heaven. To some this may seem a difficult, mystical, even misty conception; but it is, after all, only a statement in general terms of that which is true to everyday experience. Why does the picture of Jesus on the cross appeal to the conscience of mankind ? Not because they feel that their evil deeds have any definite causal relation to the crucifixion in history, but because in the Crucified they see the eternal relation of God to sin; not because they are beholding a transaction made in the distant past for their benefit, but because in those sufferings they catch the reflected light of an eternal truth. " God is reigning from the tree "—not two thousand years ago, in a distant part of the earth, but now and here. The love of God is timeless ; Jesus brought it into time, and wrought its golden thread into the history of human thought.

It has been the purpose of this study to suggest a philosophy of divine forgiveness, and no more. The reader will readily grasp that the matter does not stop here ; forgiveness is not only the end of alienation, but the beginning of coöperation. When there occurs between any two persons an act of forgiveness, there is infused into the person forgiven something of the spirit of the other. A new spirit, a new influence has with the forgiveness entered his life ; the sense of forgiveness brings also a sense of union and active sympathy, which must issue in newness of life. This also is a psychological affair; it is not a thing of logic, or duty, or gratitude; it is not, "You are forgiven, you must lead a better life"; it is a sequence of nature; it is the gentle touch of God, thrilling a new spirit into life.

Forgiveness is the beginning—the oft repeated beginning—of the spiritual life. It is the getting on to the road, not the end of the journey. I said just now that the emblems of the Communion were designed to keep before our minds the cost of forgiveness. But that was not all. When Jesus was asked, "How can this man give us his flesh to eat?" his answer was, "It is spirit that quickens; flesh profits nothing. The words that I use (flesh and blood) mean spirit and life." It is the spirit and life of Jesus that every Christian must absorb and assimilate. God's love is the sun which gives us life; forgiveness is the first sense of warmth that steals over us when we come out into the sunshine. Forgiveness and life are not separate things; they are all of a piece. Forgiveness is the introduction to that union with the Divine in which salvation consists; the cost of salvation is the cost of forgiveness.

Again, in this essay I have only sought to show in what sense the life and death of Jesus is to be regarded as a sacrifice for sin; I do not forget that it is also an ensample to us of godly life. This is, indeed, only another aspect of the same thing; for if, in the drama of his costly forgiveness, Jesus exhibited to us the mind, the nature and the love of God, it was in order that that mind should also be in us, that love should possess us, that nature should become ours. Exactly in proportion as we perceive the life of Jesus to be the revelation of God, just so can the example of Jesus be a moving force in our lives. To him we are debtors, not only for the revelation of God's life, but for the continuous inspiration of our own.

Lastly—and this is merely a tentative suggestion—it may be that as Jesus was the revealer, on the one side, of God to man, so on the other he was, in a sense, the revealer of men to God; not, indeed (which were absurd), by adding anything to the knowledge of God, but by penetrating, as man, more completely into the depth of God's personal cognition.

Perhaps this is the true meaning of "taking of the manhood into God," and might help us towards a better understanding of those figures of "priesthood" and "intercession" which have played so considerable a part in Christian literature.

Whatever be the destiny of future thought, we have at least reached the end of hypotheses of Atonement by Satisfaction, and we may find a new contentment—possibly even a complete solution of the problem—in Atonement by Self-Revelation.

There I must leave it. The vista opened up to our thought is a large one, full of variety and colour; its exploration I must leave to the reader. My object has been to lay before your minds, as clearly as may be, what appears to mine to be the principle of forgiveness both in God and man; how it implies and is based on suffering; and how suffering, such as God can undergo, is rooted in love. Only by the path of suffering can love win through to forgiveness. It behoved the Christ to suffer, because he had to manifest God to men; because he had to reveal to man the way in which God has to forgive—the only way.

# CHAPTER VIII

I DO not conceal from myself that the method by which I have interpreted the sufferings of Christ differs widely from the methods in common use. To this initial handicap is added the difficulty which has been felt in stating my case. For, while I have attempted to shape it in the form of an argument, yet it has not presented itself to my mind in terms of logic. I have seemed rather to see the thing as a living picture of a divinely human process; this picture I have but endeavoured to describe. If my words carry any conviction, it will be because the process I seek to describe is alive. For this very reason it is out of harmony with the lifeless, commercial and forensic thought of the past.

The perspective is entirely altered; it is as though I see through a stereoscope what has

formerly been to me a flat field ; to understand
the effect of a stereoscope, one must look
through it.    Yet I must try, as best I may,
to explain the change which it brings about,
as enhancing, not perverting, the vision of
things.

The death of Christ has been commonly
regarded, not as of a piece with the rest of his
life, not as the culminating point of his revelation of God, but as existing, as it were, in
theological isolation ; a thing by itself ; a bright
point of light, throwing its dazzling ray across
space and time, and finding itself, so to speak,
reflected in the eye of God, rather than having
its source in Him.    Such a view is to me
frankly impossible ; the theological isolation is
unthinkable.    Christ is the light that lightens
every man ; yet the rays, which give us light,
are all derived from the primary Sun.    The
love of Christ is that which warms the heart of
man ; yet it is but a manifestation in time of
the timeless love in the heart of God.

Jesus is fitly described as the express image
of the person of God ; the whole process of his
thought and action had its eternal archetype
and original in the person of the Almighty

Father; from this universal statement we cannot isolate his sufferings; he was still doing that which he had seen with his Father. The interpretation which I have adopted in no way tends to evacuate Christ's passion of its specific potency; for that potency is the potency of the passion of God, projected on to the screen of human life.

But, you may say, by this explanation the significance of Christ's death is wholly symbolical; it is not the ultimate thing. Yet, though it be not the whole ultimate thing, it still may be, and is, a bit of it; though it be a symbol, yet it is a vital part of that which it symbolises.

The sufferings of Christ bear the same relation to the sufferings of God as the life of Christ bears to the life of God. The one is an expression and a part of the other. Call it a symbol if you will. In a sense the life of Christ is a symbol of the life of God. The rocket fired from the shore is the symbol of safety to the sinking ship; but it is an effectual symbol; it brings the safety which it symbolises. It is not the whole of the ultimate thing; yet it, and it alone, makes available to the ship the forces which are concentrated on the shore.

So, I take it, if Christ be the incarnate God, he is the effectual symbol of all that is available for man in the heart of the Eternal; effectual, because the life of Jesus is God's living thought expressed to man. Let us beware that we do not stifle truth with words; a symbol, thus defined, may be the very heart of reality.

For all who believe in the Incarnation, the whole life of Christ is the manifestation of the life of God. For me, the passion of Christ is the climax of his life, and is the manifestation of the passion of God. The interpretation to which I point involves no departure from the faith of the Incarnation; it postulates, while it explains, the necessity of Christ's suffering; and it shows a living relation between man the sinner, and God the Sufferer.

But more than this too. For this interpretation will convey a meaning even to those who feel unable to profess a faith in the actual Incarnation. For such men, all the commercial and forensic theories have no meaning. To these I offer this explanation as a symbolism of truth; not to them indeed an effectual, but

a suggestive symbolism. They cannot believe
that Jesus was God ; but nearly all believe
that he was very like what God must be. To
such men, I think, this sort of teaching may
prove intelligible. Though they cannot find in
Christ the Incarnate God, yet they may find in
him the way to the Father ; for a Father who
suffers and forgives is a Father in whom they
can believe. Of such men and women there
are multitudes, and they are very near the
kingdom of heaven ; nearer, I say, by far, than
many who render easy lip-service to the doctrine
of the Incarnation. I am not of their num-
ber, but I know many of them my spiritual
superiors. The difference between our points
of view is the difference between effectual and
suggestive symbolism. To the one Jesus is like
the divine, to the other he is divine.

Once again, it may be objected that I have
represented Christ as bearing and forgiving the
sins of the men with whom he came in earthly
contact, so that other men are referred back
for their forgiveness away from Jesus to God
the Father. Yet Christ did nothing for the
men of his own time that he does not do for
us ; to them and us alike he brought by his

life the message of God's forgiving love ; and
I know not what more there was to do.
Through him alone we and they alike re-
ceive it.

I have devoted a few words to save my
thesis from misrepresentation.  Yet it is not
my object to reinforce, as it were, an elaborate
edifice of argument ; my only desire is to en-
able others to see clearly the living picture as
I have seen it ; and, alas, the attempt to describe in words a vital process seems almost
fatuous.  I can but present it to the best
of my ability, in the hope that the description
may conjure up the picture to other minds.

For, indeed, I cannot but feel that such
an interpretation of the passion of Christ, if
it should find acceptance, would exercise an
incalculable influence for good, not only on
the Church in particular, but on the world in
general.

First, the world.  I am convinced that men,
thoughtful men, are deterred from a frank acceptance of Christianity far more by reason of unmoral, unspiritual, untheological hypotheses of
atonement, which seem to them bound up with the
Christian religion, than by any actual difficulty

in accepting, in itself, the religion of the Incarnation. Give them a moral and spiritual
view of the atonement, in touch with reason,
nature, and psychology, and the other difficulties
will appear, not indeed insignificant, but in
their proper perspective.

If now, the passion of Jesus be regarded
as an unveiling of the heart of God, a recital
before humanity of the music of the divine
mind, and *not* as an artifice or plan to alter that
mind, or to change the motive of that music—
then, I am convinced, one of the most powerful
causes of antipathy against the Christian belief
will have been removed. My experience may
be exceptional, but I have certainly met many
thoughtful men whose minds stick, not at the
thought of an Incarnation as such, but at the
irrational and unspiritual ideas of atonement
which seem to them inseparable from it. That
the current views of the Atonement should have
produced such an effect, I consider natural
and inevitable ; their correction will no less
naturally and inevitably draw men back towards the Christian faith. If, for instance, the
Incarnation be—as it still is in the popular
mind—in the main the harbinger of a scheme

of Atonement which leaves much to be desired in its ethics and psychology, the tendency must be, and undoubtedly is, to reject the Incarnation, not on its own merits, but on the demerits of its supposed object. You cannot make an appeal to thoughtful men on behalf of Christianity, unless you remove from its substance all that grates on sound moral instinct. A man's religion cannot clash with his ethics. A thorough reconstruction of our theory of divine forgiveness must be effected before Christianity can come into its own. The faith which overcomes the world must be a faith whose roots are bedded deep in, and ramify through, the soil of our moral consciousness. I earnestly commend these few words to the consideration of all who desire to impart religious teaching, whether to men, women, or children.

But if a doctrine of divine forgiveness, which is in touch with life, would have a Christianising effect on the outside world, much more would it tend to obliterate the artificial differences which have sprung up within the Church. For while all admit that Jesus indicated a close connexion between his passion and the forgiveness of sins, yet no clear distinction has been drawn between this fact and the corollary of a penal or quasi-penal satisfaction.

As a consequence, the self-styled evangelical adheres to the substitution theory—watered down, indeed, to meet modern exigency, yet still in essence the same; the ethical school, on the contrary, rejects this hypothesis as artificial, unmoral, and even mythical; while they lay stress on the effect of the love of God in Christ on the human heart, as it appeals to the religious emotion and instinct, yet they shrink from defining any process within the heart of God which may have made forgiveness possible. The result is, that one party within the Church is maintaining a theory which the other rejects. What now if the theory in question be a mistaken conclusion, wholly unjustified by the premisses? What if the need for suffering be an internal psychological necessity, inherent in the relation of forgiver to forgiven—a necessity not only independent, but exclusive of any external or forensic interpretation? This, I think, is a matter to be pondered by the Evangelical mind. To those, on the other hand, who lean to the ethical and emotional, as opposed to the theological view, I would suggest : What if this necessary suffering within the heart of God, be the very thing —as it is—which creates the subjective response within the heart of man ? If these things be so, then, in the philosophy of forgiveness which I have outlined, there may be found, not a compromise between two opposing views, but a common platform, on to which both parties may mount from opposite sides, and so find themselves on a higher level of common faith and mutual understanding.

I have endeavoured to shew that there is no divergence between Christian religion and Christian ethics. Their apparent opposition has created a real difficulty ; and I have attempted a real solution. Shall we be told that such a solution lacks authority, or that it differs from the view which the Church has held in ages past ? The answer is twofold. No authority has put forth any comprehensive theory of the Atonement ; hypothesis has succeeded hypothesis, each forced on by the felt inadequacy of the preceding ; at the present time, there is not even a hypothesis which can be said to hold the field. But even if authority were all against such a solution, authority is not a force which binds our thought, but which educates our intelligence. The mind of each age trusts its great thinkers ; but another generation is heir to the thought of the past, and superadds its own contribution ; if it were not so, then in every sphere of thought humanity would stagnate and progress would end. Again, we may be told that New Testament writers held no such theory. I admit it. It is neither the philosophy of the Pauline Epistles, nor even—explicitly at least—of the fourth Gospel : but it is in general accord with the spirit of all, and does not run counter to any of the main features of their religious faith. The Pauline philosophy is not the Johannine ; the New Testament, as a whole, contains no general philosophy of religion ; each age has its own philosophy, and each generation must think for itself—our own not less but more than others.

The last half-century has witnessed a revolution of thought which dwarfs even that of the Reformation period. The work of science has forcibly altered our entire outlook on the world. It has revolutionised our view of history; it has forced us into a new philosophy of life. We have swung round to quite another point of view, deeper, fuller, and truer than that which we have left behind. Our religious outlook must needs participate in the change; for we cannot divide our mind into watertight compartments.

Through science the whole world has become to us, not indeed understood, but intelligible; and with this has come the conviction that our religious faith too, must come to be expressed in intelligible terms. This is the task of our generation; woe to us if we do not face it with a reverent courage.

# EPILOGUE

I HAVE said that each age has its own philosophy of religion. To some this may seem a hard saying; yet it is true. The foundation, indeed, of all Christian philosophy must always be the love of God; but the foundation is not the superstructure. We cannot continue to live in the spiritual houses of our ancestors; like material houses, they need adaptation, or even, in the long course of time, reconstruction.

Every man's religious philosophy is the house in which he lives, and from which he takes his outlook on the world. This edifice is his real home. To it he returns in his quiet hours. He, and he alone, knows its every nook and cranny, its attractions and its inconveniences. Of such houses, whether they be good or bad, and of those who live in them, consists the City of God in this world.

And it is well called a City; for it bears a

close analogy to the houses of brick and mortar
which we build for our bodies. Each kind of
City has its architects, and each its history of
architecture, varying in every age with the
needs and aspirations of its citizens.

In this City all of us live who have any
religion at all. During our early years most of
us live in our parents' houses; later on, some
of us inherit and live on in them; they may not
be modern, but they are generally solid, or at
least less flimsy than the jerry-built house in a
modern street. But if we live in these older
houses, we must keep them fresh; we must
have enough windows to let in the light of
modern knowledge, and open too, to admit the
fresh air of modern thought. In these old
houses there is a special danger of insanitary
conditions; dry rot, damp, and drainage all
have their spiritual counterparts.

On account of the inconvenience, and often
the ugliness, of the older houses, many of us
prefer to build new dwellings; but here also
we encounter difficulties. Good architects are
few; and unless we can be our own architects,
we must choose our adviser with care. In
these days houses are built in rows, without

attention to the special requirements of the individual; you must take it or leave it. And
with the best architect, you will have to check
his design to your own need; it is you, not he,
who will have to live in the house. Well then,
you say, let us each build on our own plan.
But here also, beware. If you wish to be
your own architect, you must study architecture; otherwise you will be leaving out the
staircase.

In spite of drawbacks, the citizens are all
housed somehow; many of them are dissatisfied
with their dwellings, yet have not the time, or
skill, or material with which to make altera-
tions; some of them flit from house to house;
but these have no abiding home. And some,
alas, live in old tumble-down houses, which are
incapable of restoration, because it is too much
trouble to move.

The City presents a vast diversity of struc-
tural style; some houses are both old and
beautiful, but now unsound; some are elaborate
modern buildings, but few of them are beautiful. The City is conglomerate of many
centuries, and its architects are of every
nation.

Storms visit the City at intervals. Great tempests came upon it some three centuries ago; since then the whole City has been rebuilt; the style was mostly new, but part was rebuilt on the old design. And now for fifty years the City has been tunnelled in all directions, and the shaking of modern traffic does not make for the stability of houses. Truly, the problems are great and difficult; yet they have to be faced squarely by the men of our generation.

In this great City, reader, you and I both have our abode. Do you live in a house inherited from your parents? See to it that it is sound and up to date, with the requirements of spiritual health. Or are you building for yourself? Then build with caution. Primarily, indeed, you are building for yourself; you are providing your own home, fixing your own outlook. Yet no man builds for himself alone; your children will be brought up in the same house, and with the same outlook; your friends too, in a lesser degree, cannot fail to experience, for good or evil, the influence of your architecture on their own.

In these pages I have tried to suggest some

principles of sound building ; I have found
them good for myself, and they may prove
useful to others. It is only with such a hope
that I send out this little book to take its
chance of catching once and again a sympa-
thetic eye, and of helping perhaps a few who
are in need of help.

For EU product safety concerns, contact us at Calle de José Abascal, 56–1°,
28003 Madrid, Spain or eugpsr@cambridge.org.

www.ingramcontent.com/pod-product-compliance
Ingram Content Group UK Ltd.
Pitfield, Milton Keynes, MK11 3LW, UK
UKHW012332130625
459647UK00009B/245